Lutheranism 101
WORSHIP

Written by
Thomas M. Winger

General Editor
Scot A. Kinnaman

CONCORDIA PUBLISHING HOUSE • SAINT LOUIS

Lutheranism 101 Books

Lutheranism 101

Lutheranism 101: **THE COURSE**

Lutheranism 101: **FOR KIDS**

Lutheranism 101: **THE LORD'S SUPPER**

Lutheranism 101: **HOLY BAPTISM**

Lutheranism 101: **All ABOUT JESUS**

3558 S. Jefferson Ave., St. Louis, MO 63118-3968
1-800-325-3040 • www.cph.org

Manufactured in the United States of America

Library of Congress Cataloging-in-Publication Data
Names: Winger, Thomas M., author. | Kinnaman, Scot A., editor.
Title: Lutheran worship / written by Thomas M. Winger ; general editor, Scot A. Kinnaman.
Description: St. Louis : Concordia Publishing House, 2017. | Series: Lutheranism 101 | Includes bibliographical references and index.
Identifiers: LCCN 2017043614 (print) | LCCN 2017045838 (ebook) | ISBN 9780758657510 | ISBN 9780758634092 (alk. paper)
Subjects: LCSH: Public worship–Lutheran Church–Textbooks.
Classification: LCC BX8067.A1 (ebook) | LCC BX8067.A1 W56 2017 (print) | DDC 264/.041–dc23
LC record available at https://lccn.loc.gov/2017043614

4 5 6 7 8 9 10 26 25

Contents

Visit lutheranism101.com to download the free Leader's Guide.

Foreword

Lutheranism 101 books give you usable and comprehensive overviews of what Lutherans believe and teach. These beliefs rest on the foundational discussions of who God is, who man is, and who Jesus is. Along the way, and because faith does not happen in isolation, the series also presents how this faith is confessed in what Lutherans do, both in their corporate practice and in their personal piety.

After the release of the original *Lutheranism 101* book, numerous questions, comments, and suggestions were received, focusing on the meeting point between faith and practice. The *Lutheranism 101* series grew out of this correspondence. Each book in the series picks one topic and explores the basics of the Lutheran teaching in that area. The author also explores practice in that area, the understanding being that one necessarily informs the other.

The very title, *Lutheranism 101*, points forward to the learning and building up of the Christian faith through study and by participation in the Divine Service. *Lutheranism 101* encourages the use (and, dare we say, acquisition) of the basic resources for a Christian's study and growth: a Bible, Luther's Small Catechism, a hymnal, and, ultimately, the Lutheran Confessions.

All over the world, Lutherans gather to worship. We do so to receive the precious gifts our Lord desires to give us: the forgiveness of sins, life, and salvation. Again and again, He comes into our midst with this treasure as the Gospel is preached and read, as the Absolution is spoken, as people become His children through Holy Baptism, and as His true body and true blood are distributed and received in His Holy Supper. The hymns, prayers, and praises of the congregation are always in response to God's gracious acts. First the Lord delivers, and then the congregation praises Him for it. Lutheran worship is a continual conversation between God and the believer, in which we focus on Jesus, who is present with and for us through His Word and Sacrament. *Worship* expands on the topic from *Lutheranism 101*, presenting background information on the development of Lutheran worship, a deeper look at the parts of the worship service, and an understanding of why Lutheran worship is both consistent with the way Christians have worshiped over the centuries as well as a unique expression of Lutheran theology.

Each chapter concludes with several questions that can be used to further the study of and discussion about the material. For those who may be leading a group discussion based on these chapters and for those individuals who want to check their answers against the author's comments, a free downloadable guide is available online at lutheranism101.com.

Abbreviations

AE	Luther, Martin. *Luther's Works*. American Edition. Volumes 1–30: Edited by Jaroslav Pelikan. St. Louis: Concordia, 1955–76. Volumes 31–55: Edited by Helmut Lehmann. Philadelphia/Minneapolis: Muhlenberg/Fortress, 1957–86. Volumes 56–82: Edited by Christopher Boyd Brown and Benjamin T. G. Mayes. St. Louis: Concordia, 2009–.
KJV	King James Version
LSB	*Lutheran Service Book*. St. Louis: Concordia, 2006.
Lutheranism 101	Kinnaman, Scot A., gen. ed. *Lutheranism 101*. St. Louis: Concordia, 2010.
LW	*Lutheran Worship*. St. Louis: Concordia, 1982.
TLH	*The Lutheran Hymnal*. St. Louis: Concordia, 1941.

Lutheran Confessions

You will see many quotations from the Lutheran Confessions as found in the Book of Concord. The following list provides abbreviations used, what they mean, and examples of how you would find the text. Unless otherwise noted, the English translations of the Lutheran Confessions cited in this book come from *Concordia: The Lutheran Confessions*, 2nd ed. (St. Louis: Concordia, 2006).

AC	Augsburg Confession
Ap	Apology of the Augsburg Confession
BEC	A Brief Exhortation to Confession
Ep	Epitome of the Formula of Concord
FC	Formula of Concord
SA	Smalcald Articles
SC	Small Catechism
SD	Solid Declaration of the Formula of Concord
Tr	Treatise on the Power and Primacy of the Pope

Examples:

AC XX 4	(Augsburg Confession, Article XX, paragraph 4)
Ap IV 229	(Apology of the AC, Article IV, paragraph 229)
FC SD X 24	(Solid Declaration of the Formula of Concord, Article X, paragraph 24)
FC Ep V 8	(Epitome of the Formula of Concord, Article V, paragraph 8)
LC V 32, 37	(Large Catechism, Part V, paragraphs 32 and 37)
SA III I 6	(Smalcald Articles, Part III, Article I, paragraph 6)
SC III 5	(Small Catechism, Part III, paragraph 5)
Tr 5	(Treatise, paragraph 5)

NAVIGATING LUTHERANISM 101

WHAT DOES THIS MEAN?

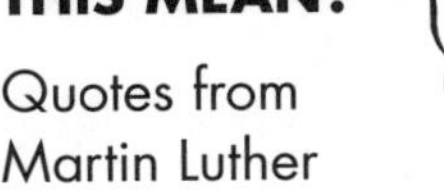

Quotes from Martin Luther

MAKING CONNECTIONS

Connecting theology, faith, and life

NEED TO KNOW

Terms and phrases quickly defined

FROM THE BIBLE

Quotations from, well, the Bible

TECHNICAL STUFF

Big theological concepts in bite-size pieces

BELIEVE, TEACH, CONFESS

Quotations from the Lutheran Confessions

INTRODUCTION

God Calls Us to This Place

A Holy Place

The great cathedrals of Europe inspire a hushed silence as visitors crane their necks toward the stone vaults above and their eyes follow the richly colored light falling gloriously into the cavernous space below. Words and music resonate with an other-worldly grandeur. Every nook and cranny is filled with sculptures, each wall decked with art. Saints and angels peer down on puny pilgrims snaking through the sacred space to the high altar. Is it any wonder that we're awestruck by such a place?

The ancient faithful who raised these glorious buildings were remarkably skilled with stone, glass, and wood. They created spaces that move hearts toward God—spaces that simply feel sacred. But for all their grandeur, these cathedrals aren't holy because of the way they look and feel. They're holy because something goes on there that doesn't happen anywhere else on earth. Yet, truth be told, the holy thing that happens there also goes on in your church, whether grand or simple. That's what this book is all about.

FROM THE BIBLE

And when the priests came out of the Holy Place, a cloud filled the house of the LORD, so that the priests could not stand to minister because of the cloud, for the glory of the LORD filled the house of the LORD. (1 Kings 8:10–11)

A Place for Worship

Many people today are seeking God, looking for a spiritual experience. They jump from church to church, from religion to religion. Some think they can find God by looking inside themselves through meditation. Others find an experience of God in nature and think they can worship Him anywhere. This quest is universal, for God has planted in the hearts of His created people a longing to find Him (Psalm 27:8). But where is God to be found?

In New Testament times, the Jews and their neighboring cousins, the Samaritans, disagreed on the answer. Was God to be worshiped in Jerusalem or on Mount Gerizim? In John 4, a Samaritan woman tried to get Jesus to take sides in the argument. The Old Testament gave a pretty clear answer, and Jesus at first implied that the Jews were right (John 4:22). But *why* were they to worship Him only in Jerusalem?

FROM THE BIBLE

You shall go to the place that the LORD your God will choose, to make His name to dwell there. (Deuteronomy 26:2)

When Solomon was permitted to build a glorious temple in Jerusalem, God showed His approval by filling it with His glorious presence (1 Kings 8:10–11). But God didn't come to the temple because Solomon called Him. Rather, *God called Solomon* to worship Him in that place. He chose that place for His name to dwell (Deuteronomy 26:2; 1 Kings 9:3). And that's why they were to worship Him there.

So Jesus' puzzling answer to the Samaritan woman is both new and old: "The hour is coming, and is now here, when the true worshipers will worship the Father in spirit and truth" (John 4:23). What's new is that since Christ has come, true worship is no longer restricted to Jerusalem. But the place of worship is really still the same. It's where God chooses to dwell with us. It's where God calls His people by His Spirit through the truth of His Word. And so it's where Jesus is, for He *is* the truth (14:6).

Like the lost sheep in Jesus' parable (Luke 15:4–7), we end up in dire straits if we run off looking for God. But Jesus the Good Shepherd calls out to us and finds us, lifts us on His shoulders, and brings us into His fold. This sheepfold is the Church, the place where God is present for us with His gifts. There He speaks tenderly to us, feeds us, and protects us.

WHAT DOES THIS MEAN?

It is one thing if God is present, and another if he is present for you. He is there for you when he adds his Word and binds himself, saying, "Here you are to find me." Now when you have the Word, you can grasp and have him with certainty and say, "Here I have thee, according to thy Word." (AE 37:68)

God Calls Us into His House

The Divine Service (the chief service of preaching and the Lord's Supper) of the Lutheran Church begins with this call: "In the name of the Father and of the Son and of the Holy Spirit." This Invocation tells us what's going on. Imagine the most intimate family gathering in your home, perhaps Thanksgiving or Christmas dinner. Just as the meal is about

FROM THE BIBLE

For where two or three are gathered in My name, there am I among them. (Matthew 18:20)

to begin, there's suddenly a knock at the door. A stranger is standing there, and you're about to send him packing. But then he tells you his name, and you realize he's part of your family, a cousin you haven't seen in years. You embrace him warmly and invite him into your house.

That's what God is doing. At the start of the service, we speak the name of our divine family, "In the name of the Father and of the Son and of the Holy Spirit," and God acknowledges us as His own. He opens the door, and He calls us into His house to dine at His festive Table. We received that holy name from our heavenly Father when we were baptized (Matthew 28:19) and reborn into a new family; and Jesus promises that He is present where His brothers and sisters gather in His name (18:20).

BELIEVE, TEACH, CONFESS

The Church is the assembly of saints (Psalm 149:1) in which the Gospel is purely taught and the Sacraments are correctly administered. (AC VII 1, author's translation)

A Sacred Space for a Holy People

Beautiful and inspiring spaces can move our hearts to worship. But what truly makes a church holy is the name that announces God's presence. As His family name, those trinitarian words create a home for God's children. God's Holy Word is proclaimed in Scripture and sermon, making the church a sacred space. Jesus presides at the Table as He once did at the Last Supper, leading the fellowship meal of God's family in His house.

That same trinitarian name made us holy when it was first placed on us in Baptism, making us God's children. The English word *saints* simply means "holy people"—and that is what we are. So the Church, properly speaking, isn't the building but God's saints (1 Corinthians 1:2). Yet we aren't the Church in isolation from one another. The Church is the gathering of the saints to hear the Gospel proclaimed and receive God's Holy Sacraments (11:23–26, 33). The Church is sheep listening to the voice of the Good Shepherd (John 10:27; SA III XII 2).

So the building is still important. The English word *church* comes from *kyrios*, which means "Lord." The church building is the "Lord's house," and the Church is the "Lord's people." The two go together because God's people need a place to gather—not to listen to one another, but to listen to Him.

We Are a Spiritual Temple

When St. Paul wrote that we have been built up into "a holy temple in the Lord" and "a dwelling place for God by the Spirit" (Ephesians 2:19–22), he meant that God's people are a living temple. What was true of the great edifice in Jerusalem is now true of us: God is truly present to give us His gifts of forgiveness, life, and salvation. We are like "living stones" in the new spiritual temple, called together by God to offer the spiritual sacrifices of prayer, praise, and thanksgiving (1 Peter 2:1–10).

This is the goal of Christ's redeeming work. He has purchased us to be God's people so that we might "live under Him in His kingdom, and serve Him in everlasting righteousness, innocence, and blessedness" (SC II 2). In other words, we are called to worship.

Study Questions

1. What makes a church building sacred or holy?

2. Can we worship God anywhere? How do we know where to find Him?

3. What does it mean to be "saints"? What is the "Church"?

Discussion Questions

1. What is the most impressive church building you have ever visited? Why did it affect you? What features of your own church building can help you be well prepared for worship?

2. How is the Divine Service like a family gathering? How is it different?

3. Read 1 Kings 8:1–10, 27–30. What made the temple a holy place? How and why did God dwell there?

4. Discuss what you know about the temple in Old Testament worship. Read 1 Peter 2:1–10. How do you think the Christian church takes the place of the temple?

PART ONE

What you'll learn about:

- The biblical basis for Christian worship in the Old Testament, in Jesus' earthly ministry, and in the writings of His apostles
- What comes first in Christian worship: God's presence and gifts to us
- How Christians respond to God's gifts in prayer, praise, and thanksgiving
- How the words we use can help us understand what's happening in worship

God Calls Us to Worship

Pagan religions invent worship to try to please their false gods. But Christian worship is given to us by God in His Holy Word. Even today, the Divine Service begins when God calls us into His presence. Worship begins not with us but with Him.

CHAPTER 1

God Called His People of Old

In This Chapter

- Understanding God's gifts in Old Testament worship
- Recognizing the presence of God with His people Israel
- Seeing how Old Testament worship points to Christ

MAKING CONNECTIONS

The hymnal can be a helpful resource for personal devotions because when creating it, the Church worked together to collect rites, hymns, and prayers that are pleasing to God.

BELIEVE, TEACH, CONFESS

God only approves services set up by His Word, which are of benefit when used in faith. (Ap XXVII 69)

Self-Chosen Worship?

Many of Jesus' most heated debates with the Pharisees centered on acts of worship. When they criticized His disciples for eating without first performing a ritual handwashing, Jesus condemned the Pharisees, saying, "In vain do they worship Me, teaching as doctrines the commandments of men" (Matthew 15:9). The Pharisees thought they could please God (worship Him) through their invented customs, but Jesus warns that self-chosen acts of worship are "in vain," or useless.

If we create our own worship, we can have no confidence that it's pleasing to God (Ap XV 17). False worship includes not just idolatry, that is, worshiping a *false* god (Deuteronomy 12:2–4; Romans 1:22–25), but also worshiping the *true* God in the *wrong* way (Deuteronomy 12:31). Because of our sinful nature, we want to do things to make God happy with us. This is the worship of the Law (Colossians 2:20–23). To learn how to worship the true God in the *right* way, the way of the Gospel, we need to turn to His Word. Holy Scripture teaches us the divinely instituted and God-pleasing way of worship.

The Old and the New

Christians today belong to the New Testament. Christ fulfilled and ended the temple sacrifices with His death on the cross, but we can learn much about the true worship of God by reading His commands to His Old Testament people. For although worship in the Old Testament took place before Christ, it was *true* worship of the *true* God. And Jesus taught us that the Old Testament Scriptures point to Him (Luke 24:44; John 5:39).

TECHNICAL STUFF

Testament (or *covenant*) refers to the promise of God to His people to forgive their sins. Jesus sealed the promise with His death and gave His body and blood in a "new testament" for us. See 2 Corinthians 3 and Hebrews 9.

The Tabernacle and Temple

When Moses came before Pharaoh in Egypt to demand the release of God's people from slavery, he first asked permission for them to go into the wilderness to *worship* (Exodus 5:1). After all, God's ultimate goal in freeing the Israelites was to restore His worshiping community in the Promised Land. In their forty years of wilderness wandering, they learned how to worship. That's what the Law recorded by Moses in the Pentateuch (the first five books of the Bible) is mostly about.

God gave Moses directions for making a lavish tent called the tabernacle, which would be carried by the Israelites and set up at the center of every encampment. Outside the tabernacle was an altar of sacrifice and a basin for washing. (See Exodus 25–31.) In the tabernacle's "Holy Place" was the altar of incense, the table of the bread of the Presence, and the lampstand. In the "Most Holy Place" was the ark of the covenant (containing the Ten Commandments, Aaron's rod, and a jar of manna [Hebrews 9:4]).

FROM THE BIBLE

It shall be a regular burnt offering throughout your generations at the entrance of the tent of meeting before the LORD, where I will meet with you, to speak to you there. There I will meet with the people of Israel, and it shall be sanctified by My glory. (Exodus 29:42–43)

The Tabernacle

The new religious observances taught by Moses in the desert centered on rituals connected with the tabernacle, and amplified Israel's sense of separateness, purity and oneness under the Lordship of Yahweh.

A few desert shrines have been found in Sinai, notably at Serabit el-Khadem and at Timnah in the Negev, and show marked Egyptian influence.

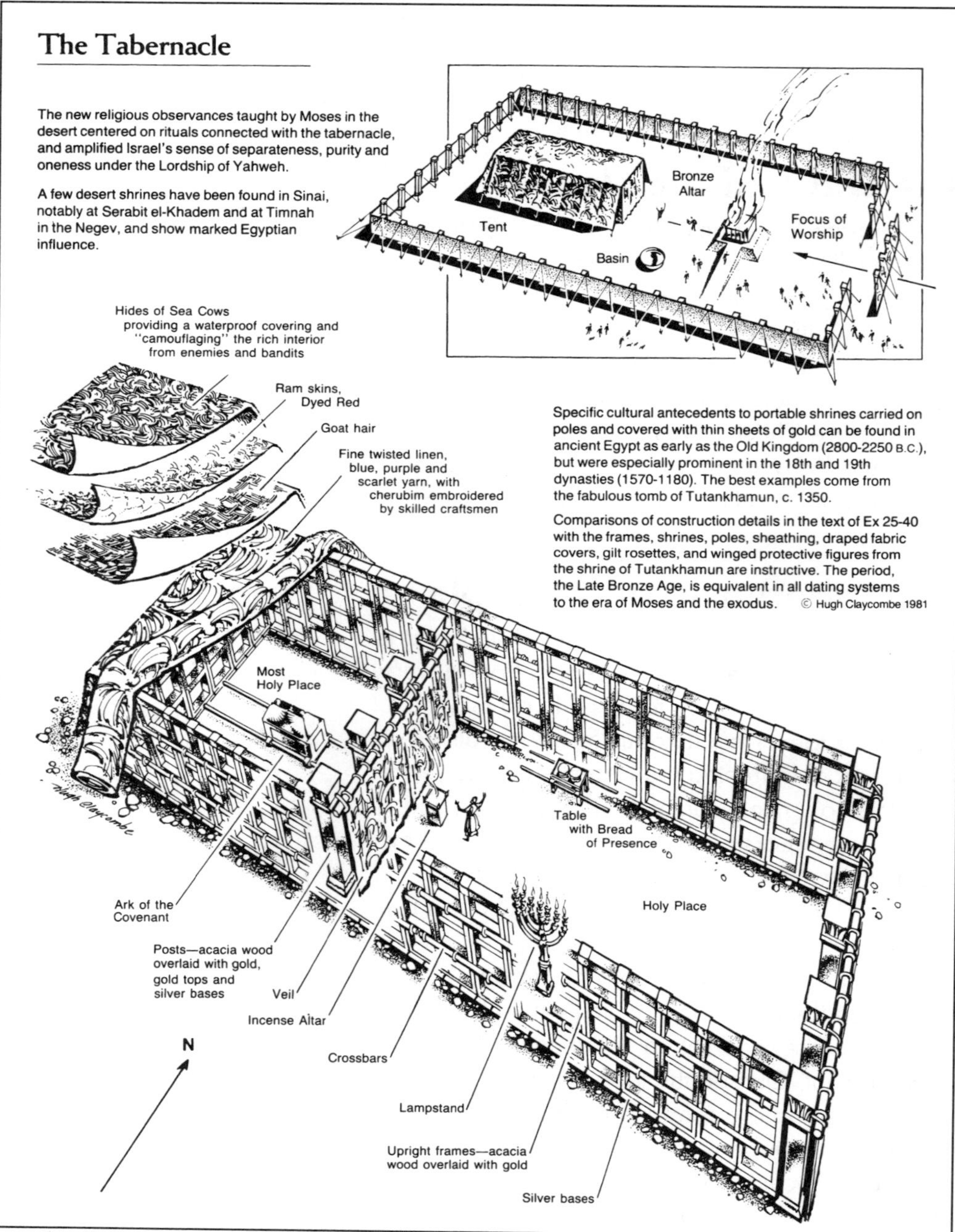

Specific cultural antecedents to portable shrines carried on poles and covered with thin sheets of gold can be found in ancient Egypt as early as the Old Kingdom (2800-2250 B.C.), but were especially prominent in the 18th and 19th dynasties (1570-1180). The best examples come from the fabulous tomb of Tutankhamun, c. 1350.

Comparisons of construction details in the text of Ex 25-40 with the frames, shrines, poles, sheathing, draped fabric covers, gilt rosettes, and winged protective figures from the shrine of Tutankhamun are instructive. The period, the Late Bronze Age, is equivalent in all dating systems to the era of Moses and the exodus.

The tabernacle was called the "tent of meeting" because God would come to speak with Moses and His people there (Exodus 29:42–43). The ark of the covenant was topped by the "Mercy Seat," the place where the invisible God was enthroned to be with and speak to His people through Moses and, later, the high priest (25:22). But God also visibly descended in a cloud of glory to show Israel that He was present in their midst to lead them and receive their worship (40:34).

When Israel entered the Promised Land, King David brought the ark of the covenant to Jerusalem, and God permitted his son Solomon to build a permanent temple to house it. The worship of the tabernacle continued in this magnificent temple. Every morning and afternoon, the priests with their Levitical assistants led a Divine Service on behalf of Israel. These daily services included

- the priestly sacrifices: a male lamb as a whole burnt offering, together with a grain and drink offering;
- pouring out the blood of the lamb on the altar for the cleansing of the people;
- priestly prayers;
- burning incense on the altar of incense to accompany the prayers;
- psalms of praise and thanksgiving by the Levites;
- eating the sacrificial banquet in the courts of the temple (God's priestly people having fellowship with Him); and
- the priestly blessing of the people with Aaron's benediction (Numbers 6:22–26).
- Later Jews added recitation of the Ten Commandments and a creedal statement known as the "Shema" (Deuteronomy 6:4).

FROM THE BIBLE

Let my prayer be counted as incense before You, and the lifting up of my hands as the evening sacrifice! (Psalm 141:2)

FROM THE BIBLE

The LORD spoke to Moses, saying, "Speak to Aaron and his sons, saying, Thus you shall bless the people of Israel: you shall say to them, The LORD bless you and keep you; the LORD make His face to shine upon you and be gracious to you; the LORD lift up His countenance upon you and give you peace." (Numbers 6:22–26)

Through this worship, God promised to be with His people, to make them holy, and to bless them (Exodus 29:42–46).

The Festivals

In addition to this daily worship, God instituted a series of annual festivals. Every man in Israel was required to be present at the Jerusalem temple for these "holy convocations" (Exodus 23:14–17; Leviticus 23). These festivals had three functions:

- They reminded God's people of His great saving deeds in the past, particularly their rescue from slavery in Egypt.
- They reminded Israel of God's ongoing gifts through the land and gave them opportunity for thanksgiving.
- They pointed forward to an even greater rescue to be enacted by the coming Messiah.

1. Passover took place on the fourteenth day of the first month (in spring). A perfect male lamb or goat was slaughtered at the temple, then roasted whole and consumed during a large family gathering at home. The meat was accompanied by unleavened bread and bitter herbs. Together with the stories that were told by the head of the household, the Passover reminded Israel of their rescue from slavery in Egypt. It was followed by the **Feast of Unleavened Bread**. Having thrown out the old leavening lumps, the people ate only unleavened bread for seven days. At its conclusion, they gave thanks during the **Feast of Firstfruits** for the firstfruits of the grain harvest (barley) with sacrifices and offerings.

2. The **Feast of Weeks** or **Pentecost** took place seven weeks (a Sabbath of Sabbaths), or fifty days, after Passover (*Pentecost* means "fiftieth"). This was a thanksgiving for the fullness of the grain harvest (wheat), and included both animal and grain offerings to God. Its date coincided with Israel's appearance before God at Mount Sinai (Exodus 19:1) and thus was a remembrance of His giving them the covenant.

3. The **seventh month** contained a series of high festivals marking this "Sabbath of months." After the **Feast of Trumpets** came the **Day of Atonement**, when the high priest entered into the Most Holy Place to sprinkle blood on the Mercy Seat for the forgiveness of Israel's sins. Finally, they celebrated the **Feast of Booths**. Taking tree branches, they constructed shelters in which to live for seven days while offering sacrifices and rejoicing before the Lord. This was a reminder of Israel's sojourn in the wilderness and included thanksgiving for the autumnal fruit harvest and new wine.

TECHNICAL STUFF

A *type* (meaning "pattern") is a person, event, or institution in the Old Testament that foreshadows or prophesies Jesus Christ, the Church, or heaven above. See Romans 5:14; Hebrews 8:5; 1 Peter 3:21.

Each of these great festivals revealed its deeper meaning with the coming of Jesus Christ. The New Testament sees the exodus as a "type" or prophecy of the redemption from slavery to sin and the devil, which Jesus achieved through His death and resurrection.

The Sabbath

For the average Israelites who couldn't attend the daily service of the Jerusalem temple, the Sabbath was the moment of worship that most often touched their lives.

The Hebrew word *Sabbath* means "ceasing" or "resting." When God gave the Third Commandment, He explained that it was a remembrance of creation (Exodus 20:8–11). Just as God "worked" for six days and then "rested" on the seventh day (Genesis 2:1–3), so His people Israel were to work six days and refrain from work on the seventh. "Closed on Saturday" became the distinctive mark of the Jews.

But the Sabbath was never simply about cultural identity or finding a balance between work and play! Although obeying the Third Commandment brought the blessings for this life that God attached to it, the Sabbath had three deeper, spiritual purposes.

1. Worship: The Sabbath was the day for a "holy convocation"—a gathering of God's people at the temple for worship (Leviticus 23:3). The daily sacrifices were doubled (Numbers 28:9–10) and the Word of God was proclaimed. But also, in every household of the land, and wherever Israelites were scattered in the world, they were to rest on the Sabbath and devote themselves to studying His Word and prayer. So Luther was quite right when he explained the Third Commandment as a call to heed God's Word proclaimed in public worship.

BELIEVE, TEACH, CONFESS

Luther's explanation of the Third Commandment: "We should fear and love God so that we may not despise preaching and His Word, but hold it sacred, and gladly hear and learn it." (SC I 3)

2. Messiah: The Old Testament only hints at the prophetic meaning of the Sabbath. But it was clearly meant to prepare Israel for something—Someone—yet to come. God promised King David that his son would be a "man of rest." This promise was partly fulfilled in Solomon, the peaceful king who would build God's temple. But it was ultimately fulfilled in Jesus, the Son of David who would build an eternal house and bring eternal rest (1 Chronicles 22:6–10).

3. Eternity: As we saw above, the Sabbath principle was applied to many parts of Israel's liturgical calendar, as weeks, months, and even years were on a

FROM THE BIBLE

So then, there remains a Sabbath rest for the people of God, for whoever has entered God's rest has also rested from his works as God did from His. (Hebrews 4:9–10)

cycle of sevens (see also Leviticus 25). This was a hint that the history of the world itself was heading toward an eternal Sabbath (Hebrews 4:9–10). Each week when God's people rested from their labors and listened to His Word, they were enjoying a foretaste of the eternal rest of heaven itself, eternal worship.

Daily Prayer

The Old Testament tells us that God's people prayed three times a day. The psalmist cries out "evening and morning and at noon" (Psalm 55:17), and we see Daniel observing these daily prayers facing Jerusalem (Daniel 6:10). Why those times and this orientation? Through their prayers, the Israelites participated spiritually in the sacrifices and prayers that were taking place at those times at the temple (9:21). By turning toward Jerusalem to pray, Israelites throughout the land remembered that God was in their midst and that the sacrifices and prayers performed in Jerusalem were for them also.

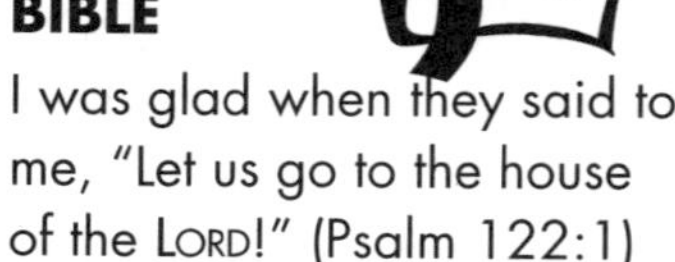

FROM THE BIBLE

I was glad when they said to me, "Let us go to the house of the Lord!" (Psalm 122:1)

Psalms and Choirs

Although God doesn't give explicit commands for the use of the Book of Psalms in worship, this "hymnal" of the Bible was written and collected primarily for public worship (Psalm 122:1). The introductions to the Psalms often tell us the liturgical occasion for which they were written.

King David himself, under the inspiration of the Holy Spirit, organized the Levites at the temple not only as priests but also as choirs and troops of instrumental musicians (1 Chronicles 23–25). This latter division stood on the steps of the temple to sing psalms and make music to lead the people's thanks and praise during the sacrifices. The psalms were a central part of Israel's worship. They also held an important place in the synagogue service and private prayer.

Synagogue

The synagogue is not found in the Old Testament and was not instituted by God. But by New Testament times, it was a central part of Jewish life. It probably developed during the Babylonian exile (sixth century BC), when the temple had been destroyed and the people were cut off from its worship. A synagogue could be formed wherever there were ten Jewish men. Synagogue buildings were simple, with benches along the sides and an open space in the center where the Scripture scrolls were kept in a box and brought out for reading and teaching.

TECHNICAL STUFF

The Greek word *synagogue* means "gathering together." The word *congregation* (from Latin) has a similar meaning.

The synagogue was an extension of the Sabbath and was created so that Jews could devote themselves to God's Word and prayer on that day. Services also took place on new moons, feast days, and Mondays and Thursdays. Interestingly, the earliest account of a synagogue service is in the New Testament, where Jesus is handed the scroll of Isaiah to read and He sits down to teach (Luke 4:16–21). Paul tells us that the Torah of Moses was read in the synagogue (2 Corinthians 3:15), and Paul was often asked to preach there (Acts 13:15).

FROM THE BIBLE

Hear, O Israel: The LORD our God, the LORD is one. (Deuteronomy 6:4)

From later writings of Jewish rabbis, we are able to piece together that the elements of a typical synagogue service included the following:

- reciting the "Shema" creed (beginning with Deuteronomy 6:4);
- eighteen prayers called "benedictions," which began, "Blessed are You, O LORD, our God";
- if a priest was present, the Aaronic benediction (Numbers 6:22–26);
- Scripture readings from the Pentateuch and the prophets;
- preaching or teaching;
- psalm singing; and
- final prayers.

Since Christianity often grew out of synagogue communities, it is not at all surprising that early Christians kept many of these elements in their worship, particularly in daily prayer and the Service of the Word.

Study Questions

1. What was the main purpose of the tabernacle? What occurred in its daily services?

2. What were the three major festivals of the Old Testament liturgical calendar? What three functions did they serve?

3. What were God's people Israel supposed to do on the Sabbath?

4. How did the synagogue originate? What did Israelites at the time of the New Testament do in the synagogue?

Visit lutheranism101.com to download the free Leader's Guide.

Discussion Questions

1. Review the layout of the tabernacle on page 18. What do you think God was teaching His people through its arrangement into various sections divided by walls and curtains?

2. Read Hebrews 9:1–14 (and vv. 15–28, if you have time). What did Jesus do to make the divisions of the old tabernacle obsolete? What does Jesus still do for us?

3. Discuss the significance of the fact that Jesus instituted the Lord's Supper, died on the cross, and rose from the dead *during the Feast of Passover.*

4. Think about how the observance of Sunday as a day of rest has changed in your lifetime. Are the changes good or bad? What is the danger when Christians think of the "Sabbath" (whether Saturday or Sunday) simply as a day when they shouldn't work? Review Luther's explanation of the Third Commandment (*LSB*, p. 321).

5. Review the description of worship in the synagogue. Compare it to the Service of the Word in one of the settings of the Divine Service in *Lutheran Service Book*. How do you think the synagogue affected Christian worship?

CHAPTER 2

God Called His New Testament People

In This Chapter

- Seeing Jesus as the fulfillment of Old Testament worship
- Recognizing the presence and work of Jesus in Christian worship
- Receiving the way of worship from Jesus and His apostles for today's Church

The New Testament doesn't give us a complete order of service in all its details. But it's a mistake to think that it has nothing to tell us about Christian worship. We Christians cling to Christ and His words. So we turn to the New Testament to learn how the worship of God's people was transformed by Jesus and to receive the gifts He has instituted for us.

Jesus and the Old Testament

There are two common misunderstandings of the Old Testament that can lead us to ignore its worship. One is the idea that the Old Testament is just *Law* (commandments), while the Gospel comes only in the New. The other is the idea that the Old Testament merely makes an occasional *prophecy* about the coming Messiah, but otherwise is not really a Christian book. This means that the temple has nothing at all to do with Christ.

But St. Paul argues that God's Old Testament people were justified by faith in the coming Messiah (Romans 4), not by works of the Law. And Hebrews carefully argues that the temple, its priesthood, and its sacrifices were all pointing forward to Christ.

Jesus Himself began His great Sermon on

TECHNICAL STUFF

The word translated "law" in our English Bibles is *Torah* in Hebrew or *nomos* in Greek. It really means "teaching" (Law and Gospel), and sometimes refers to the five Books of Moses.

the Mount by saying, "Do not think that I have come to abolish the Law [Torah] or the Prophets; I have not come to abolish them but to fulfill them" (Matthew 5:17). What He's saying is that the way of God with His people in the Old Testament doesn't simply end but reaches its true meaning in Him.

Jesus accomplishes what the Old Testament couldn't ultimately do: He saves people from their sins. The Old Testament sacrifices were performed in the weak flesh of humans and animals, but Jesus' flesh has divine power (Romans 8:3–4). Paul calls the old rituals and festivals "a shadow of the things to come" (Colossians 2:16–17). This means that they were *like* Christ, but they had no power apart from Him, their "substance." The Scriptures from beginning to end—not just in certain prophecies—proclaim Jesus (John 5:39; Luke 24:44).

Jesus and the Temple

The Gospels describe Jesus' relationship to the temple in two ways. On the one hand, Jesus saw it as His Father's house and regularly worshiped there. On the other hand, He announced its eventual destruction, to be replaced by His own flesh.

Jesus Views the Temple as His Father's House

Jesus most certainly knew that God was everywhere. And yet He chose to visit the temple courts regularly for worship, teaching, and prayer. His actions confess the importance of God's *gracious* presence in the temple to give out His gifts and receive Israel's praise.

FROM THE BIBLE

Why were you looking for Me? Did you not know that I must be in My Father's house? (Luke 2:49)

Jesus first appeared at the temple to be circumcised and presented to the Lord as Mary's firstborn son (Luke 2:21–39). But unlike all other firstborn sons of Israel, Jesus wasn't redeemed by a five-shekel payment (Numbers 18:16). Like Samuel, who was given into God's service in the temple (1 Samuel 1:22), Jesus was dedicated to the Lord, and so He saw the temple as His home.

This explains Jesus' words and actions when He was twelve years old and His earthly parents couldn't find Him among the pilgrims leaving Jerusalem after the Passover; it was natural that He would be in His Father's house (Luke 2:49).

As an adult, He continued to visit the temple, faithfully observing its festivals, as John's Gospel particularly emphasizes (e.g., 2:13). Jesus used the temple courts and its sheltered colonnades to teach His disciples and the crowds. He embodied God's presence in the temple for His people.

Jesus Replaces and Fulfills the Purpose of the Temple

But on Jesus' final visit to the temple with His disciples at the beginning of Holy Week, shortly before His death, He pointed to the temple's massive stones and proclaimed their destruction (Matthew 24:1–2). Historically, this happened in AD 70 when the Romans destroyed Jerusalem. But it had already happened more profoundly in Jesus' ministry.

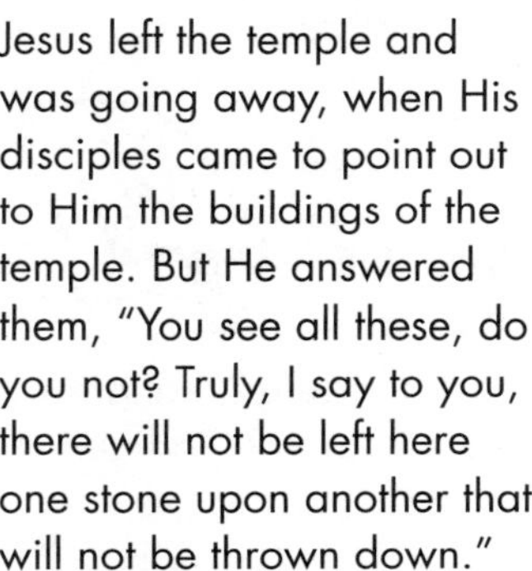

FROM THE BIBLE

Jesus left the temple and was going away, when His disciples came to point out to Him the buildings of the temple. But He answered them, "You see all these, do you not? Truly, I say to you, there will not be left here one stone upon another that will not be thrown down." (Matthew 24:1–2)

John's Gospel teaches us that Jesus replaces and fulfills the purpose of the temple. He begins by telling us that the Son of God "became flesh and *dwelt* among us" (1:14). The Greek word for "dwelt" literally means "tented" or "tabernacled." It means that God's Son took on human flesh to be more fully what the tabernacle and temple had been: God's dwelling place among His people.

The destruction of the temple would be a picture of Jesus' death, but only Jesus' body would be raised up (John 2:19–21)—the temple was no longer needed. Jesus proclaims about Himself, "Something greater than the temple is here" (Matthew 12:6). The question whether to worship on Mount Gerizim or Jerusalem no longer mattered (John 4:20–24). The temple had been the place where lambs were slaughtered to redeem Israel from death, but now Jesus was the Lamb who bore their sins (1:29). The temple had been the place to receive life-giving water from God, but now people should come to Jesus and drink (7:37–39). The temple had been the way to the Father, but now it was Jesus (14:6).

FROM THE BIBLE

The next day he saw Jesus coming toward him, and said, "Behold, the Lamb of God, who takes away the sin of the world!" (John 1:29)

Jesus Is the High Priest and the Sacrifice

The Letter to the Hebrews digs deeper and shows us that Christ is the meaning of *everything* that went on in the tabernacle/temple. He is greater than the temple priesthood, "A high priest forever after the order of Melchizedek" (Hebrews 6:20). Jesus didn't inherit His priesthood like the sons of Aaron but claimed it by right as the eternal Son of God.

FROM THE BIBLE

He has appeared once for all at the end of the ages to put away sin by the sacrifice of Himself. (Hebrews 9:26)

FROM THE BIBLE

Since we have a great priest over the house of God, let us draw near with a true heart in full assurance of faith, with our hearts sprinkled clean from an evil conscience and our bodies washed with pure water. (Hebrews 10:21–22)

FROM THE BIBLE

But you are a chosen race, a royal priesthood, a holy nation, a people for His own possession, that you may proclaim the excellencies of Him who called you out of darkness into His marvelous light. (1 Peter 2:9)

Jesus, then, doesn't need to offer sacrifices for His own sins before He can sacrifice for the sins of others (7:27). Nor does He need to offer sacrifices over and over again (9:25–26). His self-sacrifice on the cross counts once and for all for the sins of the world.

Hebrews teaches that everything we saw in the earthly temple was merely a copy of a better, heavenly sanctuary. The most important feature of the temple was the gracious and glorious presence of God, who is visibly present in heaven. And once Jesus had offered His eternal sacrifice, He sat down in the heavenly sanctuary, His work complete (Hebrews 10:12). So Jesus' ministry is "better" than the Old Testament's, founded on "better promises" (8:6).

But even though His sacrifice is complete, Jesus hasn't stopped working for us. In the heavenly sanctuary, He remains our High Priest, interceding before the Father's throne (Hebrews 7:25; 8:1–2). Through Him, we have access to the King of the universe (4:16). Through Him, we can draw near to the heavenly Father as children who are cleansed by Holy Baptism and have a pure heart (10:19–22). And in the heavenly sanctuary, He continues to lead the worship of the heavenly hosts and His Church on earth.

Jesus Leads a Priestly People

So "priesthood" isn't done away with in the New Testament, but, like the temple, it's transformed. There are no longer Levitical priests offering physical sacrifices in Jerusalem. But Jesus, the great High Priest, works through the pastoral ministry He instituted to bring the fruits of His sacrifice to His people. And Jesus leads His people's response to these gifts. He leads the worship of all God's people, who are a "kingdom of priests" (Exodus 19:6). This great privilege that once belonged to Israel alone is now extended to all nations.

This is made possible by the cleansing and sanctifying water of Holy Baptism, which gives birth to a priestly people. By uniting them with the great High Priest—Jesus Christ—Baptism leads God's people into His intimate presence, giving them access to His throne of grace. These baptized priests offer their very bodies as living sacrifices to God (Romans 12:1). They offer sacrifices of praise and thanksgiving, proclaiming in the Divine Service the saving deeds of God (1 Peter 2:1–10).

In this way, Jesus builds a new, Spirit-filled temple, whose stones are alive because they've been raised to new life with Him through Baptism (Ephesians 2:19–22). So the New Testament pictures the Church as the fulfillment of the temple, as God's worshiping community.

Jesus and the Sabbath

FROM THE BIBLE

And He came to Nazareth, where He had been brought up. And as was His custom, He went to the synagogue on the Sabbath day, and He stood up to read. (Luke 4:16)

FROM THE BIBLE

Come to Me, all who labor and are heavy laden, and I will give you rest. (Matthew 11:28)

Jesus' relationship to the Sabbath and synagogue worship was similar to His relationship to the temple. On the one hand, Jesus faithfully attended the Sabbath services in the synagogue (Luke 4:16). He taught in the synagogue, listened to God's Word, and prayed there.

But Jesus' relationship to the Sabbath itself was quite explosive! When He healed people on the Sabbath or allowed His disciples to pluck grain, the Pharisees accused Him of breaking God's Law (Matthew 12:1–14). Sometimes we think that Jesus was merely showing the Pharisees a more merciful way to observe the Sabbath, exposing them as legalists. But there was more going on.

Jesus reminds them that King David ate the bread of the Presence in the tabernacle on the Sabbath, even though this was only lawful for priests. Was He suggesting it's okay to break God's Law if you have a good reason? No, Jesus was hinting at the fulfillment of the Sabbath. David could do this because he was a living prophecy (a "type") of Christ, the Son of David. The story teaches us that the true meaning of the Sabbath, to enjoy rest in the house of God and in His presence, was fulfilled when the Messiah came.

For Jesus Himself is the Sabbath's fulfillment. He brings true rest (Matthew 11:28). False gods rest while men serve them. But our God works for us so that we might share in His rest (see the Third Commandment, Exodus 20:8–11). In the Old Testament, the temple was that place of rest (1 Kings 8:56; Psalm 132:8). Because of their unfaithfulness, Israel failed to enter the promised rest (Hebrews 4:1–11). But God's rest is ours if we listen to the words of Jesus and live with Him (vv. 10–11; SC I 3). This is why the disciples can't be judged for plucking grain on the Sabbath—for they are with Jesus! And every time we are with Jesus by His holy name, His Word, His body and blood, we have that Sabbath rest.

Jesus Teaches and Prays

As Jesus drew disciples to Himself, He taught them, prayed for them, and trained them to pray. In this way, He began the worship of the New Testament in His own ministry. And by taking these actions into the homes of His people, Jesus paved the way for Christian house churches everywhere. Worship would take place wherever Jesus Himself was present through His name and Word (Matthew 18:20).

FROM THE BIBLE

Sanctify them in the truth; Your word is truth. . . . I made known to them Your name, and I will continue to make it known, that the love with which You have loved Me may be in them, and I in them. (John 17:17, 26)

A great illustration of this is the story of Mary and Martha (Luke 10:38–42). Martha's loving desire to feed and serve her Lord is admirable, but Jesus commends Mary for choosing something better: she sat at His feet and listened to His teaching. This gave Jesus great joy, because He came not to be served but to serve (Mark 10:45). His three-year ministry leading up to His sacrificial death was filled with His teaching.

When He had finished His teaching, Jesus often withdrew from the crowds to pray. The climax of His prayer life came on the eve of His crucifixion. In the Upper Room, after teaching His apostles and instituting His Supper, He prayed the great "High Priestly Prayer" (John 17). He prayed that His disciples would know the Father and receive eternal life, that they would be preserved from the attacks of the devil, and that they would remain united in God's Word and name. He then went out with them to the Garden of Gethsemane and threw Himself into agonized prayer, looking ahead to His death (Matthew 26:36–46). He prayed that the Father's will would be done in His sacrificial death.

All that Jesus taught about prayer is tremendously important, beginning with the prayer He taught in the Sermon on the Mount (Matthew 6:5–15). The prayer He taught us, beginning "Our Father," is a precious gift to the Church as it gives us words that we know are pleasing to our heavenly Father and teaches us how to pray. But more important yet is that Jesus prayed for His Church and still prays for her as He leads her worship before God's throne.

FROM THE BIBLE

Now Jesus was praying in a certain place, and when He finished, one of His disciples said to Him, "Lord, teach us to pray, as John taught his disciples." And He said to them, "When you pray, say: 'Father, hallowed be Your name.'" (Luke 11:1–2)

Jesus Forgives Sinners and Eats with Them

As the Pharisees were angered by Jesus' treatment of the Sabbath, so, too, were they offended by the company He kept. For He had the habit of entering the homes of tax collectors and sinners, even to dine with them (Mark 2:15–17). Table fellowship was deeply meaningful to traditional Middle-Eastern societies, particularly to Jews. His eating with sinners implied to the Pharisees that Jesus approved of their behavior—and surely their sinful uncleanness would rub off on Him.

But the Pharisees got it backward. When Jesus ate with sinners, His holiness rubbed off on *them*! He didn't approve of their sins but forgave them, giving them a gift that only God can give. "Your sins are forgiven," He says to the sinful woman; "Your faith has saved you; go in peace" (Luke 7:48–50).

This great gift was available to those who ate with Him because of who He was. Like the elders of Israel who dined in the presence of God Almighty on Mount Sinai (Exodus 24:11), like the Israelites who ate the fellowship meals in the temple, these blessed sinners eating with Jesus were in the presence of God Himself.

With these meals, Jesus was creating the worship of the New Testament. He was teaching, forgiving, and sharing Table fellowship with His people, house by house, in meals that would soon reach their climax in the Supper He would institute.

FROM THE BIBLE

And the scribes of the Pharisees, when they saw that He was eating with sinners and tax collectors, said to His disciples, "Why does He eat with tax collectors and sinners?" And when Jesus heard it, He said to them, "Those who are well have no need of a physician, but those who are sick. I came not to call the righteous, but sinners." (Mark 2:16–17)

Jesus Institutes the Means of Grace

As John admits at the close of his Gospel, Jesus did and said so many things that, if he were to write them all down, the whole world could not contain the books (John 21:25)! How are we to know what Jesus wants His Church today to continue doing?

At the end of all four Gospels, Jesus prepares His apostles for His ascension by answering this very question. The Church isn't left guessing about what Christian worship will look like when Jesus is no longer visibly with them. Jesus delivers to His apostles the authority to do what He had been doing:

- **Baptism:** make disciples by baptizing them in the name of the Holy Trinity and teaching them to cling to all that Jesus said (Matthew 28:19–20);
- **Preaching:** preach repentance and the forgiveness of sins to all nations (Luke 24:47);
- **Absolution:** forgive the sins of the penitent and retain the sins of the impenitent (John 20:23); and
- **Lord's Supper:** deliver the precious body and blood of Jesus in the Sacrament of the Altar (1 Corinthians 11:23–26).

FROM THE BIBLE

If you abide in Me, and My words abide in you, ask whatever you wish, and it will be done for you. (John 15:7)

We call these the "Means of Grace" because they are the ways in which the gracious gifts of forgiveness, life, and salvation are delivered to God's people. These gifts themselves are the substance of Christian worship. And so Christian worship is given to us by Christ's "mandate"—His Word of command that includes the authority to do what He bids.

So Jesus' Word is central to Christian worship in more than one way. Of course, we read His words and deeds from the four Gospels in the Divine Service. But we also read His mandating Word with each Means of Grace. Jesus' Word gives life-giving power to Baptism, Absolution, preaching, and the Supper. In this way, Christian worship is centered on Jesus' Word.

Together with these fundamental gifts, Jesus institutes prayer to the Father in His name (John 16:23). The prayer He taught us, which begins "Our Father," is the most perfect example. We pray in response to hearing God's Word, and He promises to hear us (John 15:7). But prayer is intertwined through the whole of Christian worship and reaches its climax in the prayer of thanksgiving that responds to the great gift of the Lord's Supper (Ephesians 5:20).

If we follow Jesus' words and do what He has commanded, we know that our worship is pleasing to the Father—not because our work is worth it, but because Jesus' sacrifice was pleasing to the Father (Ephesians 5:2). Our worship is acceptable to God because it is offered through Him (1 Peter 2:5).

The Apostles Do What Jesus Gave Them to Do

When Jesus instituted these gifts, He asked one thing of His apostles: faithfulness. He promised that if they clung to all that He had entrusted to them, He would be with them (and us!) to the end of the age (Matthew 28:20).

FROM THE BIBLE

For I received from the Lord what I also delivered to you, that the Lord Jesus on the night when He was betrayed took bread. (1 Corinthians 11:23)

The apostles—whose name means "sent [by Jesus]"—carried out their mission by teaching the Church to do what Christ gave them. And so the earliest Christians devoted themselves to the apostolic teaching, broke bread, and prayed as Christ had mandated (Acts 2:42). Paul turned the early Gentile Christians from the worship of idols to the true worship of God through Christ (1 Thessalonians 1:9). He did this by handing on what Jesus gave, such as instructions concerning the Lord's Supper that had first been given to him (1 Corinthians 11:23).

Paul tells Timothy to read the Scriptures to the gathered congregation, to preach to and teach them (1 Timothy 4:13). He instructs Timothy to lead a "general prayer" for all in authority and for the salvation of all people (2:1–4). He calls for a worship that is full of psalm-singing and thanksgiving (Ephesians 5:19–20).

As the apostles carry out what Jesus gave them to do, as they teach churches to worship according to Jesus' mandate, a pattern is set for the whole Christian Church. We'll look at the way our liturgy grows out of the words of Jesus and the apostles in more detail below.

A Foretaste of Heaven

The biblical story of worship moves from the Old Testament to the New, from Jesus through the apostles to the Church of all time. But it doesn't end here on earth.

The revelation granted to John draws back the veil to show the worship of the heavenly hosts before the throne of God. There the Lamb who was slain and now lives eternally leads the worship of saints and angels (Revelation 4–7). We see our heavenly goal, the purpose for which God redeemed His people.

But heavenly worship isn't just for angels and saints who have departed this life.

FROM THE BIBLE

But you have come to . . . the heavenly Jerusalem, and to innumerable angels in festal gathering, and to the assembly of the firstborn who are enrolled in heaven, and to God, the judge of all, and to the spirits of the righteous made perfect, and to Jesus, the mediator of a new covenant. (Hebrews 12:22–24)

TECHNICAL STUFF

Maranatha is an Aramaic word that means either "[Our] Lord has come" or "[Our] Lord, come!" It appears in many early Communion rites and was already used in Corinth in Paul's day (1 Corinthians 16:22). It expresses the twofold meaning of the real presence in the Sacrament. (See *LSB*, p. 162.)

Because our risen Lord Jesus is still with His Church on earth through His Word and Sacraments, the Christian Church's earthly worship is already joined to its heavenly counterpart. We have already come to the heavenly Jerusalem (Hebrews 12:22–24).

This reality is most clearly expressed in the Lord's Supper, which not only anticipates the eternal banquet but also joins us to the heavenly feast here and now. When we receive Jesus' body and blood, we are feasting with the saints and angels above. Jesus taught His disciples that His Supper pointed to the heavenly kingdom (Luke 22:16). St. Paul reminds us that the angels are present with us in worship (Ephesians 3:10).

Each time the Christian Church gathers around Jesus' Word and Supper, we urgently expect His return, praying, "Our Lord, come!" (1 Corinthians 16:22). And on that Last Day, the veil will be drawn back and we will see our Lord in His glory, the One who was always with us and who will lead us into the eternal worship of heaven.

Study Questions

1. When and how did Jesus participate in temple worship during His earthly ministry?

2. Read John 2:18–21. What was Jesus saying about the temple?

3. What are the privileges and responsibilities given to all Christians as God's *priestly* people?

4. Did Jesus uphold, break, or fulfill the Sabbath?

5. What did Jesus do in His own ministry that set a pattern for Christian worship?

6. Why is it significant that the apostles carried on doing what Jesus gave them to do?

Discussion Questions

1. Jesus prophesied the destruction of the temple, which took place in AD 70 when the Romans destroyed Jerusalem. Discuss what this did to Jewish worship and how God might have used it to drive people to Christ.

2. Read Hebrews 8:1–7. In what ways is Jesus' priesthood and sacrifice "better" than those in the Old Testament?

3. Read or sing *LSB* 530, "No Temple Now, No Gift of Price." Discuss how Jesus fulfilled and replaced every aspect of temple worship.

4. Read Mark 2:15–17. Discuss the deep significance of Jesus' meals with sinful people.

5. Read Exodus 24:1–11. In what ways does the Lord's Supper fulfill this great event? How do both meals point to the heavenly banquet?

Visit lutheranism101.com to download the free Leader's Guide.

6. Read Hebrews 12:22–24 and Revelation 5:11–14. Discuss the significance of the fact that heaven is pictured as a place of eternal *worship*. What does the Book of Hebrews imply when it says, "You have come to . . . the assembly of the firstborn who are enrolled in heaven" (12:22–23)?

CHAPTER 3

Understanding the Call to Worship

In This Chapter

- Understanding that *who* God is defines *how* we worship Him
- Recognizing that God's gifts to us come before we respond in prayer, praise, and thanksgiving
- Learning how the words we use confess what's going on

We've seen how important it is to start with Scripture, to learn from God's Word what acts of worship are pleasing to Him. In the Divine Service itself, God also takes the initiative. He doesn't wait for us to come to Him, but He calls us into His house, prepares us to be in His presence, speaks to us in His Word, and feeds us with His nourishing sacramental gifts. In response to such goodness, how can we not thank and praise Him and ask Him for help in our every need!

Need to Know

The Athanasian Creed is one of three ancient creeds included in our Lutheran Book of Concord (the other two are the Apostles' and the Nicene Creeds). It was probably written at the end of the fifth century and reflects the teachings of St. Athanasius, who was at the Nicene Council in AD 325. The Athanasian Creed may be found on page 319 in *Lutheran Service Book*.

Trinitarian and Christological

It's a tradition in most Lutheran churches to confess the Athanasian Creed on Trinity Sunday. It's a long statement of faith that hammers out in great detail the relationship between the three persons in our one God.

But this creed isn't just about doctrine. It describes the God whom we worship. It emphasizes the glory and majesty of God's nature that leads us to praise Him. We can only worship Him if we know Him.

The Athanasian Creed has two parts; it

BELIEVE, TEACH, CONFESS

The Athanasian Creed begins, "Whoever desires to be saved must, above all, hold the catholic faith. Whoever does not keep it whole and undefiled will without doubt perish eternally. And the catholic faith is this, that we *worship* one God in Trinity and Trinity in Unity, neither confusing the persons nor dividing the substance." (*LSB*, p. 319)

discusses (1) the three persons of the Holy Trinity and (2) the two natures of Jesus Christ. This teaches us that true Christian worship must always be both trinitarian and Christological.

It is *trinitarian* in two ways. The Father, Son, and Holy Spirit is the true God we worship. This is woven into the entire liturgy of the Divine Service, especially in the repetition of the Gloria Patri ("Glory be to the Father, and . . ."). So there is no true worship of just God the Father, or Jesus alone, or only the Spirit. The Trinity is also the *way* we worship God. The Holy Spirit leads us to faith in Christ through His Word, and Christ brings us to the throne of God the Father.

This worship is possible only because of Jesus' work, and so our worship is always *Christological*. Jesus opened access to the throne of God through His atoning work on the cross: "For through Him we both have access in one Spirit to the Father" (Ephesians 2:18). As we have seen from Hebrews, Jesus continues to lead the worship of God's people. And Jesus gives Himself to us in the Divine Service as His Word is spoken and His body and blood are delivered.

FROM THE BIBLE

Be filled with the *Spirit*, addressing one another in psalms and hymns and spiritual songs, singing and making melody to the Lord with your heart, giving thanks always and for everything to *God the Father* in the name of our *Lord Jesus Christ*. (Ephesians 5:18–20, emphasis added)

Cleansed to Enter God's Presence

Worship begins with God and not us because He's holy and we aren't. Even Moses, who spoke with God as with a friend (Exodus 33:11), couldn't come near God without taking off his sandals (3:5)—evoking an image of cleansing from the filth of sin. God hid His glory from Moses in the burning bush and in a cloud in the tabernacle, for no man could see God's face and live (33:20).

In the Old Testament, every priest who approached the Holy Place of God's presence in the tabernacle needed to be anointed with oil, washed with water, dressed in clean linens, and sprinkled with the blood of sacrificial animals (Exodus

FROM THE BIBLE

Peter said to Him, "You shall never wash my feet." Jesus answered him, "If I do not wash you, you have no share with Me." (John 13:8)

FROM THE BIBLE

Christ loved the church and gave Himself up for her, that He might sanctify her, having cleansed her by the washing of water with the word. (Ephesians 5:25–26)

29). In fact, the whole nation of Israel needed to be cleansed before they could come before God in worship (19:10–11). These rituals showed that sinful people can't possibly come to God unless He first prepares them.

The New Testament teaches that Christ's work not only forgives our sins but also cleanses us so that we, too, can come into God's presence. Jesus pictures this with His humble act of washing the disciples' feet (John 13:4–10). He extends this work of cleansing to all Christians by instituting Holy Baptism, the washing of water and the Word that makes the Church, His Bride, presentable to Him (Ephesians 5:26) and lifts her up to the heavenly places (2:6). This washing gives us a pure heart and enables us to approach God (Hebrews 10:22).

Only those who have been cleansed from sin are able to worship God (Luke 1:74–75). So it's quite impossible for true worship to begin with us. But thankfully, God Himself opens the way to worship before His throne by the cleansing work of His Son.

Jesus Came to Serve

The story of Jesus' washing the disciples' feet on Holy Thursday isn't just an example of humility for us to copy. For those disciples weren't just Christians; they were also apostles. On the eve of His crucifixion, Jesus was teaching them how they were to carry on His ministry. But Jesus was also demonstrating the true nature of His relationship to His disciples as Savior to the saved.

For it was in His uncopiable crucifixion that Jesus ultimately showed His servanthood. Settling an argument among those apostles about what it means to be His servant, Jesus prophesied His death for them: "For even the Son of Man came not to be served but to serve, and to give His life as a ransom for many" (Mark 10:45).

Four Stories about Worship (Mark 10)

Jesus' remarkable declaration comes at the end of Mark 10, a chapter that can be seen as a debate about worship.

It begins with the disciples foolishly trying to stop people from bringing their children to Jesus to have Him bless them (vv. 13–16). It seems the disciples thought the children had nothing to offer Jesus. But, of course, they had it backward: what mattered was what Jesus could give to these helpless members of His kingdom.

As if to offer a completely opposite example, Mark next tells us of a rich man who presents Himself before Jesus as a great prize. He thinks he can *do* something for God to earn eternal life. But Jesus sends him away sorrowful by laying on him the impossible demands of the Ten Commandments, to deflate his high opinion of himself (vv. 17–31). For even the richest man can offer God nothing that He needs.

Jesus responds to this incident by prophesying His coming death, reminding the disciples that the kingdom of God is really about what He is going to do for them (vv. 32–34). Now the disciples think they've got it, and so the sons of Zebedee come to Jesus with their outrageous demand to have seats at His right and left in the kingdom of glory. But these aren't the gifts that Jesus has promised. He offers only a cup of suffering, a baptism of death (vv. 35–45).

If you view these stories through the lens of Christian worship, things start to come into focus. Worship isn't about us having something to offer God, as if He needed us. Rather, it's about being like those little children who seek the blessing of Jesus. It's about submitting to the service Jesus wants to offer in His suffering and death.

And so Mark ends his chapter with one final encounter. Bartimaeus, a blind beggar, has nothing to offer Jesus but his cries for help. Again, the crowds don't want him to bother Jesus—but this is why He came. The beggar cries, "Have mercy on me!" and Jesus mercifully heals him (vv. 46–52). Helpless beggars are helped by Jesus. This is what goes on in the Divine Service!

FROM THE BIBLE

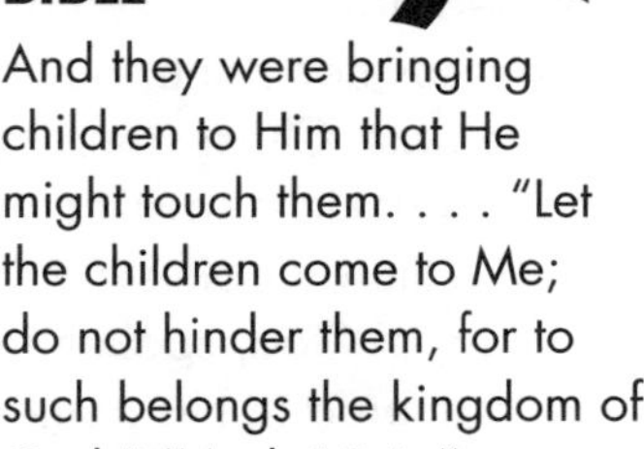

And they were bringing children to Him that He might touch them. . . . "Let the children come to Me; do not hinder them, for to such belongs the kingdom of God." (Mark 10:14)

FROM THE BIBLE

"Good Teacher, what must I do to inherit eternal life?" And Jesus said to him, "Why do you call Me good? No one is good except God alone." (Mark 10:17)

FROM THE BIBLE

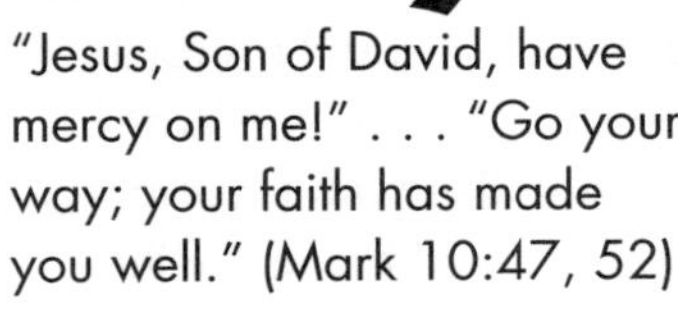

"Jesus, Son of David, have mercy on me!" . . . "Go your way; your faith has made you well." (Mark 10:47, 52)

Jesus Is Still among Us

We've come to see that, as unclean sinners, we can't possibly reach out to God. We learn from His Word how to worship Him, and we respond to the saving work that Jesus has done. But it would be quite wrong to think of Christ's work as entirely in the past. Christ came to serve not only when He gave His life as a ransom for many, but He also still comes among us as a servant.

The liturgy points continually to the real presence of Christ. It begins with the naming of God, spoken in response to Christ's promise that where two or three are gathered in His name, He is there in their midst (Matthew 18:20). The Kyrie repeats Bartimaeus's cry of "Lord, have mercy," because Christ is standing in front of *us* poor beggars as well. The Gloria in Excelsis sings angelic praise to the baby born at Bethlehem who is present in the flesh with us too. The Scripture readings are Jesus' own voice speaking to us. Through the preacher, Jesus preaches. Jesus presides at His Supper to give His body and blood to His gathered disciples. We sing "Lamb of God" *to* Him, recognizing that He is here. And He dismisses us with His own words of blessing.

We will explore these elements of the liturgy in detail below. But what unites them all is Jesus' promise to be among us as One who serves. *The whole liturgy is about the real presence of Jesus.*

WHAT DOES THIS MEAN?

We teach with the Word, we consecrate with the Word, we bind and absolve sins by the Word, we baptize with the Word, we sacrifice with the Word, we judge all things by the Word. (AE 40:21)

Worship of the Law or the Gospel?

Jesus' encounter with the rich man (Mark 10:17–22) starkly pictures "the worship of the Law." This is the way people naturally think they should relate to God. This attitude comes from the "old Adam," the sinful nature we're born with that thinks a whole lot more of itself than it ought to! The old Adam holds up his pathetic works and expects God to be pleased. But nothing short of perfection can ever please God if we approach Him through the Ten Commandments.

BELIEVE, TEACH, CONFESS

So the worship and divine service of the Gospel is to receive gifts from God. On the contrary, the worship of the Law is to offer and present our gifts to God. However, we can offer nothing to God unless we have first been reconciled and born again. (Ap V 189)

All worship is guided by and carried out with the Word of God. But the important question is *which* Word? The Word of God's Law or the Word of His Gospel? In Mark 10, Jesus continuously points people toward what *He* is doing *for them*, ultimately laying down His life as their ransom. And so He teaches us that the "worship" that most pleases Him is to let Him be our Savior, to cry out for help like the blind beggar. This is the worship of the *Gospel*.

Lutherans have expressed this understanding of worship particularly clearly in the Book of Concord. The Augsburg Confession gives a Gospel-centered, liturgical definition of the Church: "The Church is the assembly of saints in which the Gospel is purely taught and the Sacraments are correctly administered" (AC VII 1, author's translation). Even more concisely, the Apology says, "The chief service of God is to preach the Gospel" (Ap XV 42).

It's really about getting things in the right order. For only when the Gospel of Christ has had its way with us can we offer God worship that truly pleases Him. Prayer and praise flow from forgiven and transformed hearts.

Faith: The Highest Worship

What this ordering of worship means is that—quite contrary to what people often think—Christian worship is less about what we can do for God and more about what He does for us. And if God has gifts to offer in the Divine Service, then our first response ought to be to receive them. Ordinary gifts can be received in the hand, but the part of us that receives spiritual, Gospel gifts is *faith*.

Faith is the counterpart of the Gospel. God creates faith in us that's perfectly designed to receive His gifts, like hand in glove. Faith isn't so much our commitment to God as it is recognition of how much we depend on Him.

BELIEVE, TEACH, CONFESS

The woman came with the opinion that forgiveness of sins should be sought in Christ. This worship is the highest worship of Christ. (Ap V 33)

A woman once fell at Jesus' feet, weeping and wiping His feet with her hair and pouring precious ointment on them. It would seem like a great act of worship—which it certainly was. But Jesus points behind this act. She loved and worshiped Him greatly because He had first forgiven her many sins. He praises not her work but her *faith*, saying, "Your faith has saved you; go in peace" (Luke 7:50).

When a father comes home from a long trip and brings presents for his little children, what makes him happiest is to see their smiles and laughter, their joy in seeing him and receiving his gifts. So also our heavenly Father is most pleased when we joyfully meet Him and receive His gifts. Faith is the highest "worship" because it receives the forgiveness of sins. "God wants us to believe Him and to receive from Him blessings. He declares this to be true divine service" (Ap V 107).

The Rhythm of Worship

The first motion of a human heart is to push out oxygen-rich blood to give life to each part of the body. When the heart relaxes, it draws depleted blood back through the lungs to be reinvigorated. This "strong-weak" rhythmic pulse is a sign that the body is alive and well. If the rhythm gets out of whack, the body can't function properly.

The liturgy pulses with a similar rhythm. God's desire to give and our need to receive creates a certain rhythm in the Divine Service. The strong beat is God's rich delivery of nourishing gifts to our weakened souls. We breathe them in and are reinvigorated with divine life. God then draws back to Himself our appropriate response in joyful thanks and praise.

> Our Lord speaks and we listen. His Word bestows what it says. Faith that is born from what is heard acknowledges the gifts received with eager thankfulness and praise. . . . The rhythm of our worship is from Him to us, and then from us back to Him. He gives His gifts, and together we receive and extol them. (*LW*, p. 6)

BELIEVE, TEACH, CONFESS

A Sacrament is a ceremony or work in which God presents to us what the promise of the ceremony offers. . . . A sacrifice, on the contrary, is a ceremony or work that we give to God in order to provide Him honor. (Ap XXIV 18)

Sacrament and Sacrifice

A uniquely Lutheran way of describing this liturgical heartbeat is the distinction between *sacrament* and *sacrifice*.

A *sacrament* is an act instituted by Christ that delivers forgiveness through Word and sign (Baptism, Absolution, Lord's Supper). But when we look at the liturgy, we label any act by which God delivers His Gospel gifts as "sacramental"—including also the Scripture readings, the sermon, and blessings.

By *sacrifice*, we don't mean animal sacrifices; but we label as "sacrificial" any act of worship that we return to God in response to His sacramental gifts: prayer, praise, thanksgiving, and offerings. These are our "spiritual sacrifices" (Romans 12:1; 1 Peter 2:5).

The genius of the Western rite of the liturgy as

Lutherans have received and reformed it is the careful balance it achieves between these two elements. God's sacramental gifts are the strong beat that drives the liturgy, while our sacrificial responses are a beautiful and appropriate expression of thanksgiving and praise.

Prayer, Praise, and Thanksgiving

It's quite obvious that *thanksgiving* comes in response to a gift. The liturgy connects words of thanks particularly to the Lord's Supper in prayers, responses, and song before and after the Sacrament. Because Jesus Himself prayed a great prayer of thanksgiving before instituting His Supper, the Early Church referred to it as the "Eucharist," which means "Thanksgiving."

But *prayer* and *praise* also arise in response to God's gifts. We wouldn't know what to pray for and would have no confidence that God hears our prayers unless He first spoke to us. So prayer is a response to hearing the Word of God in Scripture readings and sermon. We speak only when we are spoken to. We ask for what God has promised, recalling what He has done for us (e.g., Ephesians 1:3–14).

True praise works the same way. While we can certainly adore God simply for who He is, He is most pleased when we praise Him for what He does for us. So praise, too, arises from hearing His Word. Praise sings back to our triune God His mighty deeds of salvation using the psalms and canticles He has provided for us in Scripture, or hymns based on Scripture. Such praise follows the pattern of New Testament doxologies (e.g., Ephesians 1:3; 3:20–21; Romans 16:27).

NEED TO KNOW

Canticle comes from the Latin word for "little song." It refers to songs drawn straight from the Bible, but outside the Book of Psalms, like the Magnificat. Two historic canticles (Gloria in Excelsis, Te Deum) are based on Scripture but are not direct quotations.

NEED TO KNOW

Doxology is a Greek word that means "proclaiming [God's] glory." Most New Testament doxologies give praise to the Father, to or through the Son, and sometimes in the Spirit. The Gloria Patri is the most common doxology in our liturgy. Many hymns end with a trinitarian doxology, marked in *LSB* with △, which invites the congregation to stand in praise.

Words for "Worship"

The New Testament doesn't give us one general word for "worship." It borrows many words from the Old Testament: reverence, glorify, serve, praise, bless, bend the knee. But it also simply describes what Christians did when they gathered together, referring particularly to "the Lord's Supper" (1 Corinthians 11:20 by contrast) or "the breaking of the bread" (Acts 2:42; 20:7).

Each of these expressions describes one aspect of worship. But, as we have just noted, the liturgy embraces a careful balance of both sacramental and sacrificial acts. So we ought to be careful that the words we use also embrace both parts.

Worship

Worship is far and away the most common word used by English-speaking Christians today—it's the title of this book, after all! But it can be a little misleading. At its root, it's a contraction of "worth-ship" and comes historically from a feudal society where people were required to acknowledge the "worth" of their overlords. This is what is meant even today when we refer in court to the judge as "your worship."

Certainly we ought to acknowledge God as our Lord! We ascribe to Him the greatest "worth" when we sing His praises. This is a vital part of biblical worship, usually expressed by the Greek word *pros-kyneo*, "bend the knee," as the Wise Men did before baby Jesus (Matthew 2:11) and the heavenly hosts do before God's throne (Revelation 4:10). But using the word *worship* to describe the entire Divine Service can mislead us into thinking only about its *sacrificial* side. It focuses on what we do, rather than what God does. It's like a heart out of rhythm or limping along on one leg.

Divine Service (*Gottesdienst*)

The old Latin expression *cultus Dei* was much broader. It meant something like "service of God" and included both God's service to us and our service to God, both the strong and the weak beats of the heart. Our German Lutheran forefathers translated this as *Gottesdienst*, "God's service," to get across the same idea.

In recent times, English-speaking Lutherans have tried to recover this broader idea with the phrase "Divine Service." The idea is that God serves us with His gifts in Word and Sacrament, and we serve Him by responding in prayer, praise, and thanksgiving. Never one without the other, but God always comes first.

Liturgy

The word *liturgy* expresses the same idea. This comes from an old Greek word still used by Eastern Orthodox Christians to describe the Divine Service. At the time of the Reformation, Lutherans revived the word to challenge the corrupt medieval idea that the Mass was all about our sacrifice to God.

The Greek word *leitourgia* combines two words that mean "people" and "work." But it's a mistake to explain it as "the work *of* the people." It really means "work *for* the people." In ancient Greece, it referred to gifts that rich citizens made to the community for the public good. In the Bible, it refers to the public services of the temple, where God—the ultimate wealthy patron—provides everything His people truly need through His priests (see Luke 1:23). And in the New Testament, Jesus Christ leads an even more excellent liturgy (Hebrews 8:6).

Sometimes people think of "liturgy" as a particular order of service or a formal style of worship. But though we might call our Western rite "the liturgy," the word really means something bigger and more profound. The liturgy is God's service to us in Word and Sacrament. So we really should never say "liturgies" (plural) but rather "the liturgy" (singular), which comes in various forms.

FROM THE BIBLE

But now [Christ] has obtained a liturgy that is as much more excellent as the covenant of which He is mediator is better, for it has been enacted on the basis of better promises. (Hebrews 8:6, author's translation)

BELIEVE, TEACH, CONFESS

Let us discuss the word *liturgy*. This word does not properly mean a sacrifice, but rather the public ministry. Liturgy agrees well with our belief that one minister who consecrates gives the Lord's body and blood to the rest of the people, just as one minister who preaches offers the Gospel to the people. (Ap XXIV 80)

Form and Freedom

Rite and Order

God is not a God of confusion but of peace and order (1 Corinthians 14:33, 40). There are many elements of "order" in worship that God has given us, such as the words and elements to use in the sacraments, and the respective roles of pastor and people. Some things can't be done any other way than He prescribes. We confess our sins before the Absolution is spoken (never the other way around). We proclaim God's Word to prepare people to receive the Lord's Supper (not the other way around). But God hasn't provided a complete order. of service with all the details and words that we must use.

So when the Church enacts the liturgy, she must have an order or "rite." Some elements of the rite are given by God, some are received from the Ancient Church, and some are worked out by present-day Christians. The rite is therefore partly God-given and partly man-made. Lutheran rites are inherited from the Western catholic tradition but reformed in the light of the Gospel.

WHAT DOES THIS MEAN?

As far as possible we should observe the same rites and ceremonies, just as all Christians have the same baptism and the same sacrament [of the altar] and no one has received a special one of his own from God. (AE 53:61)

TECHNICAL STUFF

The word *catholic* means in Greek "according to the whole." The "catholic Church" is Christ's Body extended through the whole world, in heaven above, and through all history. The true catholic Church holds to the "whole" of Christ's teaching as expressed in the creeds.

A church's rite is vitally important in two ways:

1. It expresses the church's *confession*. It does this by how it confesses the triune nature of God and the centrality of Christ, how it expresses the relationship of Law and Gospel in its balance of sacrificial and sacramental elements, and how it puts into practice the Word and the Sacraments.
2. A common rite also expresses and fosters the *unity* of the church. When Lutherans travel from one church to another, they ought to be able to participate fully, knowing that they're part of one worshiping community. And because the Lutheran rites are so similar to rites of other Western churches, it also expresses the true ecumenical (catholic) nature of the Church.

Ceremony and Adiaphora

Ceremony refers to the way in which the rite is conducted. It includes things like candles and crosses, postures like standing or kneeling, gestures like the sign of the cross, vestments like albs or chasubles, and musical choices like instruments or chanting.

The Liturgy: Definitions

Our churches are falsely accused of abolishing the Mass. The Mass is held among us and celebrated with the highest reverence. Nearly all the usual ceremonies are also preserved. (AC XXIV 1–2)

THE LITURGY
(broad sense)

Divinely Mandated	*Mixed*	*Human Decision*
Liturgy (narrow sense) *The Gifts*	**Rite** *The Setting*	**Ceremony** *The Manner*
Word and Sacrament	Order of Service	Music
Absolution	Law/Gospel Order and Balance	Vesture
Scripture Readings	Biblical Canticles and Texts	Posture
Preaching	Lectionary, Church Year	Gesture
Body and Blood of Christ	Hymn Texts	Movement, Location
Benediction	Music	Vessels, Paraments
		Incense, Art, Adornments
Fidelity	*Discernment*	*Charity*

Axis of Mandate (→ from Divinely Mandated to Human Decision)

Axis of Service (← from Charity to Fidelity)

BELIEVE, TEACH, CONFESS

Leitourgia, they say, means a sacrifice, and the Greeks call the Mass *liturgy*. (Why do they leave out here the old name *synaxis*, which shows that the Mass used to be the communion of many?) Let us discuss the word *liturgy*. This word does not properly mean a sacrifice, but rather the public ministry. Liturgy agrees well with our belief that one minister who consecrates gives the Lord's body and blood to the rest of the people, just as one minister who preaches offers the Gospel to the people. As Paul says, "This is how one should regard us, as servants of Christ and stewards of the mysteries of God" (1 Corinthians 4:1), that is, of the Gospel and the Sacraments. (Ap XXIV 79–80)

Nevertheless, we keep many traditions that are leading to good order [1 Corinthians 14:40] in the Church, such as the order of Scripture lessons in the Mass and the chief holy days. At the same time, we warn people that such observances do not justify us before God, and that it is not sinful if we omit such things, without causing offense. The Fathers knew of such freedom in human ceremonies. (AC XXVI 40–42)

Even the Church's canon law is not so severe that it demands the same rites everywhere. Nor, for that matter, have the rites of all churches ever been the same. Although, in large part, the ancient rites are diligently observed among us. It is a false and hate-filled charge that our churches have abolished all the ceremonies instituted in ancient times. But the abuses connected with the ordinary rites have been a common source of complaint. They have been corrected to some extent since they could not be approved with a good conscience. (AC XXI 2–5)

Our churches teach that one holy Church is to remain forever. The Church is the congregation of saints [Psalm 149:1] in which the Gospel is purely taught and the Sacraments are correctly administered. For the true unity of the Church it is enough to agree about the doctrine of the Gospel and the administration of the Sacraments. It is not necessary that human traditions, that is, rites or ceremonies instituted by men, should be the same everywhere. As Paul says, "One Lord, one faith, one baptism, one God and Father of all" (Ephesians 4:5–6). (AC VII 1–4)

Unlike some Reformed churches, Lutherans don't forbid such man-made ceremonies. Christian people are physical beings and will naturally express their worship with their voices and bodies, the craft of their hands—engaging all the senses in the holy space. It may be elaborate or simple, but there will always be some kind of ceremony.

There will almost certainly be different local customs in how these things are done. We call most ceremonies "adiaphora"—a Greek word that means "neither commanded nor forbidden by God." But adiaphora are not "indifferent" in the sense that they don't matter. They matter a lot! They can express true (or false!) worship. They can move the hearts of worshipers to receive God's gifts and praise Him with the right spirit. They can help (or hinder!) the proclamation of the Gospel. So the key is to examine questions in regard to ceremonies in the light of the Gospel and to choose ceremonies that will serve the liturgy's purpose.

Rubrics

Rubrics are the instructions given in our service books about how to carry out the individual elements of rite and ceremony. The word *rubric* comes from the Latin word for "red." In the Middle Ages, the instructions for carrying out the liturgy were written in red ink. *Lutheran Service Book* follows this tradition.

There are rubrics in the pew edition to help the lay participant know what to do at various points in the service. The pastor or liturgist has more rubrics in the Altar Book that help with his parts. There are "shall" rubrics that prescribe good or proper practice, while "may" rubrics allow for more freedom. Rubrics help the Body of Christ to act as one in worship. And like instructions that come with medicine, they can make sure that the gifts of God are received as God wishes us to have them.

Orders of Service

The Lutheran Church has one basic rite of the Divine Service (the chief service of preaching and the Lord's Supper). But over the centuries, it has been adapted for different places and needs. It moved from Latin into German and then into English.

BELIEVE, TEACH, CONFESS

We believe, teach, and confess that the community of God in every place and every time has, according to its circumstances, the good right, power, and authority to change and decrease or increase ceremonies ‹that are truly adiaphora›. They should do this thoughtfully and without giving offense, in an orderly and appropriate way, whenever it is considered most profitable, most beneficial, and best for good order, Christian discipline, and the Church's edification. (FC SD X 9)

Different translations of the texts resulted, some preserved in older English and some modernized. Sometimes the music is in classic chant tones, sometimes in a more recently composed form.

Our Lutheran service books and hymnals often have more than one setting of *the* "Divine Service." It's the same liturgy, the same gifts of God, but in different forms. Each is a variation on the Western rite of the liturgy. So also Matins and Morning Prayer are really just different settings of the same morning office, and Vespers and Evening Prayer are variations on the evening service.

This book will explain in some detail these regular public services of the Lutheran Church. There are many other rites that cannot be covered here, particularly the "occasional rites" such as Private Confession and Absolution, Baptism, Confirmation, Marriage, Burial, and Ordination. These, too, are Lutheran versions of classic Western orders.

Some churches venture beyond the orders provided in the Church's service books. They understand freedom in rite and ceremony to allow them to create their own orders that follow only the barest outline of the Western rite, if at all. Unfortunately, this little volume cannot treat the complexities of the contemporary worship debate in detail. But if you first understand the theology of the liturgy and the content of the rites we have received, you will be well prepared to move on to those tricky issues.

BELIEVE, TEACH, CONFESS

At the outset, we must again make this preliminary statement: we do not abolish the Mass [Divine Service], but religiously keep and defend it. Masses are celebrated among us every Lord's Day and on the other festivals. The Sacrament is offered to those who wish to use it, after they have been examined and absolved. (Ap XXIV 1)

The Wheel of Worship

The many orders of service in the Church aren't like a restaurant menu from which we just take our pick according to our tastes and appetite. There is, so to speak, an order to the orders.

As we've seen from the New Testament, the Lord's Supper is the central act of the Christian Church. From earliest days, Christians gathered on Sunday to hear the apostolic Word, break bread together, and pray (Acts 2:42). So also the central liturgical act of every Christian church is the Divine Service of Word and Sacrament on Sundays and festivals. It is the hub around which the Christian life revolves.

Radiating out from this hub are the spokes of daily prayer. Matins and Vespers (and the minor offices) are responses to and preparations for the chief gathering of the Christian congregation.

These spokes lead out to the rim of continuous personal prayer in the Christian's daily life. And the rubber that meets the road—the way every Christian is connected to the world, the path on which God has put them—is their vocation, where they serve God in their everyday calling. Thus, worship isn't just one part of Christian life. Worship embraces it all.

Study Questions

1. What does it mean that true Christian worship is "trinitarian" and "Christological"?

2. How is Mark 10:45 a key Bible text in explaining what goes on in worship?

3. What do we mean by "the rhythm of worship"?

4. What is the liturgical distinction between "sacramental" and "sacrificial"?

Visit lutheranism101.com to download the free Leader's Guide.

5. What does the German word *Gottesdienst* mean?

6. Does the word *liturgy* refer to an order of service, a kind of worship, "the work of the people," or what?

7. What is meant by the term *adiaphora*? How does a church decide what to do about ceremonies that God hasn't prescribed?

Discussion Questions

1. Discuss the many ways in which our Divine Service keeps the triune God at the center. Look through the setting of the Divine Service most familiar to you. Which parts are explicitly trinitarian?

2. Discuss the four stories in Mark 10. How does each encounter with Jesus teach us something about worship?

3. Melanchthon writes about the woman who washed Jesus' feet: "The woman came with the opinion that forgiveness of sins should be sought in Christ. This worship is the highest worship of Christ" (Ap V 33). Discuss how this definition of worship is so contrary to what we normally think.

4. Read the Introduction to *LSB*, pages viii–ix. Discuss how it explains and reinforces the theology of worship taught in this chapter.

5. There was a significant change in the title of our Lutheran hymnal from *Lutheran Worship* to *Lutheran Service Book*. What is the danger in using the word *worship* to describe what happens in the Divine Service? How might it help to be careful in our choice of words?

6. Discuss the benefits of having one common "rite" (order) of the Divine Service in the Lutheran Church. How can it be helpful to distinguish the "rite" from the "ceremony" of the liturgy?

PART TWO

What you'll learn about:

- Table fellowship with God in the Divine Service of Word and Sacrament
- How and why our Lutheran order of service developed as it is
- What each part of the Divine Service means and how it delivers the Gospel to us

God Calls Us to His Table

In the temple, God invited His priests to dine with Him by giving them a portion of the people's sacrifices. Jesus extended this divine Table fellowship to all Israel by eating with sinners and finally creating His Supper. Today, God continues to call His people to the fellowship of His table in His house at each Divine Service.

CHAPTER 4

The Story of the Divine Service

In This Chapter

- The origins of the Divine Service in Jesus' ministry
- How the Early Church faithfully carried out what Jesus had given
- The rich development of rite and ceremony in the Middle Ages
- The Lutheran reform and renewal of the liturgy

FROM THE BIBLE

When the Pharisees saw this, they said to His disciples, "Why does your teacher eat with tax collectors and sinners?" But when He heard it, He said, "Those who are well have no need of a physician, but those who are sick. Go and learn what this means, 'I desire mercy, and not sacrifice.' For I came not to call the righteous, but sinners." (Matthew 9:11–13)

The Breaking of the Bread

If you try to find in the New Testament a complete order for the Church's Divine Service, you'll be disappointed. But this doesn't mean that our order is completely man-made. Jesus set the pattern in His own ministry.

From the wedding at Cana (John 2:1–13) to Jesus' breaking bread with His disciples after His resurrection (21:9–14), Jesus' ministry was centered on Table fellowship. Jesus entered the homes of "tax collectors and sinners" to teach them, forgive their sins, and eat with them (Matthew 9:9–13). Jesus compared these meals with a wedding banquet, which in His parables is an image of eternal life with God (22:1–14; 25:1–13). John's Revelation gives us a glimpse of this marriage supper of the Lamb and His Bride, already underway in heaven (19:7–9).

So that we might join in that eternal banquet already now, Jesus instituted His Supper. He did this during the Passover, taking the Old Testament feast and remaking it in light of His death and resurrection. No longer does it remember the rescue of God's people from Egypt. Now it recalls the even greater exodus from sin and death that Jesus won on the cross. "Do this in remembrance of *Me*." With this command, Jesus creates the order of teaching, preaching, prayer, and eating that forms the core of the Divine Service.

After His resurrection, Jesus showed His Church how to continue this Divine Service. On Easter Day, He taught the two Emmaus disciples and revealed Himself to them in the breaking of the bread (Luke 24:13–32). That same evening, He appeared to His gathered disciples to speak peace to them and eat with them (vv. 33–49). The next week, the disciples gathered again on Sunday to remember His resurrection, and Jesus came to them speaking peace (John 20:26–29).

The Apostolic Service

After Jesus' ascension, the Jerusalem Christians continued to meet in homes to hear His teaching, pray, and receive His Supper. When three thousand people were baptized on Pentecost, the disciples met in the large public space of Solomon's Portico at the temple, presumably for teaching, prayer, and praise. But then they dispersed into homes for the Lord's Supper (Acts 2:46; 5:12). In Acts, Luke gives us the earliest description of a Christian Divine Service: "And they were devoting themselves to the *teaching* of the apostles and to the *communion* in the breaking of bread and to the *prayers*" (2:42, author's translation). Isn't it remarkable that this three-part outline of the apostolic liturgy is essentially the same as our Divine Service today?

WHAT DOES THIS MEAN?

The service now in common use everywhere goes back to genuine Christian beginnings. (AE 53:11)

The New Testament provides many other details of the service in apostolic times, including

- gathering in the name of Jesus (1 Corinthians 5:4);
- psalm and hymn singing (Ephesians 5:19);
- reading Scripture (Revelation 1:3);
- preaching based on Scripture (1 Timothy 4:13);
- creedal confessions (1 Corinthians 12:3);
- the gathering of offerings (1 Corinthians 16:1–2);

FROM THE BIBLE

Until I come, devote yourself to the public reading of Scripture, to exhortation, to teaching. (1 Timothy 4:13)

FROM THE BIBLE

For I received from the Lord what I also delivered to you, that the Lord Jesus on the night when He was betrayed took bread, and when He had given thanks, He broke it, and said, "This is My body which is for you. Do this in remembrance of Me." In the same way also He took the cup, after supper, saying, "This cup is the new covenant in My blood. Do this, as often as you drink it, in remembrance of Me." For as often as you eat this bread and drink the cup, you proclaim the Lord's death until He comes. (1 Corinthians 11:23–26)

- intercessory prayer (1 Timothy 2:1–2);
- a prayer of thanksgiving (1 Corinthians 14:16);
- exclusion of the unbaptized, the holy kiss of fellowship, and the prayer *Maranatha*, "O Lord, come!" before the Lord's Supper (1 Corinthians 16:20, 22);
- proclaiming the Words of Institution and eating and drinking Christ's body and blood in bread and cup (1 Corinthians 11:23–26);
- singing the Sanctus, "Holy, Holy, Holy" (Revelation 4:8); and
- a trinitarian blessing (2 Corinthians 13:14).

Early Church

The Lord's Day

Throughout Acts and Paul's epistles, we find Christians meeting on the evening of "The Lord's Day" (Sunday) for apostolic preaching and the Lord's Supper (Acts 20:7; 1 Corinthians 16:2). They met in the *evening* for three reasons: (1) to remember Jesus' appearances to the disciples in the Upper Room; (2) because Sunday was still a work day at this time; and (3) because the Lord's Supper was celebrated within an evening meal called the "Agape" (Love Feast).

NEED TO KNOW

"The Lord's Day" was the new name that early Christians gave to Sunday because it was the day when Jesus rose from the dead. It became their liturgical gathering day (Revelation 1:10). The Greek adjective *kyriakos* ("Lord's") is at the root of our English word *church* and was eventually applied to the building.

They met in the dining room of a wealthy patron, a Christian who opened his or her house to the church (1 Corinthians 16:19). Such houses might be renovated for worship purposes, but it wasn't yet possible to build dedicated churches.

These early Christians were under the watchful eye of Roman authorities who weren't entirely sure whether they should receive legal protection as Jews. Around AD 112, the Roman governor Pliny the Younger was persecuting Christians in Bithynia. He reported to Emperor Trajan what he had learned about Christian worship from lapsed Christians. He said they met once a week before dawn to "sing responsively a hymn to Christ as to a god." They would then go off to work and at the end of the day "assemble again to partake of food."

In an effort to suppress the Christians, Pliny forbade evening gatherings. It seems this is why Christians eventually abandoned the Agape meal and kept just the Lord's Supper itself, which they transferred to their Sunday morning gathering.

MAKING CONNECTIONS

As Christianity today faces an increasingly hostile culture, we may find ourselves increasingly looking to the Early Church for guidance. We can learn what is essential for our worship as we see how early Christians worshiped in homes but still had all the Lord's gifts and blessings.

Early Witnesses

In the first three centuries, Christianity mostly stayed under the Roman radar. Christians were extremely cautious about revealing exactly what went on in their gatherings. Pagans often misunderstood what Baptism and the Lord's Supper were and sometimes accused Christians of child sacrifice and cannibalism! But three early writings give us a glimpse of the truth.

Didache. The *Didache* claims to give the "teaching" of the apostles. Although it probably wasn't written by them, it surely comes from the first century. It describes fasting on Wednesdays and Fridays and praying the Lord's Prayer three times a day. It gives the trinitarian formula for Baptism and recommends the use of running water (a stream).

The *Didache* also provides sample prayers of thanksgiving over the bread and the wine for the minister to use at the Lord's Supper. It calls this sacrament "The Eucharist," which means "thanksgiving." It restricts participation to those who have been baptized and are holy and penitent. The prayers conclude with "Hosanna to the Son of David" and a paraphrase of 1 Corinthians 16:20–24 (with "Maranatha"). So, while there is no complete order of service, we recognize what's going on here.

Justin Martyr. In the middle of the second century (ca. AD 155), Justin Martyr wrote his *First Apology* ("defense" of Christianity). It gives the most detailed description of early Christian worship. He describes the Baptism of a convert and the celebration of the Lord's Supper that follows. He emphasizes that no one may partake of the Eucharist unless he is convinced of the truth of Christian teaching, has been baptized, and lives as Christ commands. For it is not common bread and wine but the flesh and blood of Christ, as the words of Jesus recorded in the Gospels teach.

Justin then describes the regular Sunday Divine Service. It begins with lengthy readings of Scripture from both Testaments. The presider then preaches a sermon based on the readings and prays for all Christians everywhere. They exchange the kiss of peace. The people bring bread and a cup of wine mixed with water to the presider, who offers a lengthy prayer of thanksgiving, and they answer, "Amen." He blesses these elements with Christ's words. After the Distribution, assisting ministers take elements to the sick. After the service, the presider takes gifts from the wealthier members and distributes them to needy members of the church.

Hippolytus. An early third-century (ca. AD 215) writing called the *Apostolic Tradition* is thought to have been written by Hippolytus, bishop of Rome. It describes "the tradition that has remained until now." Hippolytus describes the Divine Service on two different occasions: Baptism and ordination.

The *Apostolic Tradition* describes the Baptism of whole households: little children first, followed by men, and finally women. In some ways, it looks quite familiar—the candidates are instructed, they renounce Satan and his works, they confess the three articles of the Apostles' Creed. But some of the *Apostolic Tradition* is unfamiliar: the candidates are baptized naked and receive white robes afterward, they're anointed with the oil of exorcism and of thanksgiving, and they receive milk and honey as a symbol of the Promised Land.

MAKING CONNECTIONS

And on the day called Sunday, all who live in cities or in the country gather together to one place, and the memoirs of the apostles [the Gospels and Epistles] or the writings of the prophets [Old Testament] are read, as long as time permits; then, when the reader has ceased, the president [presiding minister] verbally instructs, and exhorts to the imitation of these good things. Then we all rise together and pray, and, as we before said, when our prayer is ended, bread and wine and water are brought, and the president in like manner offers prayers and thanksgivings, according to his ability, and the people assent, saying Amen; and there is a distribution to each, and a participation of that over which thanks have been given. (Justin Martyr, *First Apology*, 67)

When Hippolytus describes the Lord's Supper at an ordination, he gives the complete text of the presider's thanksgiving prayer—and it looks very familiar! It begins,

> The Lord be with you.
> *And with your spirit.*
>
> Lift up your hearts.
> *We have them with the Lord.*
>
> Let us give thanks to the Lord.
> *It is meet and right.*

We call this the "Preface Dialogue," and it is found in virtually every Christian rite in East and West. The presider continues with a prayer that confesses the work of salvation in Christ, includes the Words of Institution, prays for the Holy Spirit, and ends with a trinitarian doxology.

NEED TO KNOW

A "mixed chalice" of wine diluted with water was sometimes used by Jews at the Passover for the sake of women and children. Greco-Roman peoples also did so to make wine, which was expensive, last longer. Later Christians gave the mixed chalice a symbolic meaning: a picture of the divine and human natures of Christ, the union of the communicant with Christ, or the blood and water from Christ's side on the cross. Today, Lutherans do not normally add water to the wine.

Impact of Empire

The conversion of the Roman emperor Constantine is surely the most significant event in the Church's early history. In AD 312, he saw a vision of a cross with the words, "By this sign you will conquer." He marked his soldiers' shields with a chi-rho cross and went on to defeat his chief rival. The next year, he proclaimed toleration of all religions and began to favor Christianity in his empire. Six decades later, it became the official state religion.

The promise that Christianity would no longer be persecuted led to significant developments in her worship. Christians could now buy or erect buildings without fear that they would be confiscated. In the basilica—which means "royal" building—they found a perfect design. The basilica was rectangular, with rows of columns creating a large central space with two or four side aisles. At

NEED TO KNOW

The first two letters of the word *Christ* in Greek are chi (Χ) and rho (Ρ). When placed on top of each other, the resulting symbol can appear like a cross with Christ's head: ☧.

MAKING CONNECTIONS

The ceremony of the liturgy can be scaled to suit the place and occasion. Daily devotions or Communion visits to shut-ins take place in an intimate space where vestments and processions would be inappropriate. But it can still be helpful to use at least a cross and candles to remind you that Christ's presence makes any place sacred.

NEED TO KNOW

The offertory of the medieval Roman rite turned the Lord's Supper into a sacrifice: "Receive, holy Father, almighty eternal God, this unblemished offering which I, your unworthy servant, offer to you, my living and true God, for my innumerable sins, offences, and negligences; for all who stand round, and for all faithful Christians, alive and dead; that it may avail for my salvation and theirs to eternal life" (Jasper and Cumings, *Prayers of the Eucharist*, 3rd ed., 162).

one end was a raised platform in a semi-circular "apse" where imperial officials would sit to carry out their business. This was an ideal place for ministers to preside at an altar.

These basilicas were large enough for hundreds of worshipers. This spaciousness, together with the influence of imperial pomp, encouraged an increase in the ceremony of the liturgy. The ministers could process through the congregation to their places. Professional musicians could be provided.

The rite then developed, as psalms were sung during the procession and covered the movement of numerous ministers, particularly around the Scripture readings. The Sanctus was sung as the Lord's Supper was consecrated. And since Constantine made Sunday a holiday, there was more time in the liturgy for singing. Thus the fourth century began a golden age of hymn writing.

The injection of money enabled the Church to make her ministers' vestments from richer material. Bibles and vessels for the Lord's Supper could be made with precious metals and jewels. Candles and art (mosaics) multiplied.

So, while the content of the liturgy itself didn't change, the Constantinian period brought increased beauty and movement to the ceremony, and the rite grew to accommodate it.

Medieval Times: The Good and the Bad

From the fourth to the tenth centuries, the Western rite grew to include almost everything we know today.

While in the fourth century Augustine could comment that the service began simply with the Scripture readings, soon the "entrance rite" included a processional psalm (Introit) and the Kyrie, and the Gloria in Excelsis had been added. By the end of this period, the Agnus Dei was sung at Communion and the Nicene Creed was confessed before it.

In New Testament times, Greek was the Roman Empire's common language. Latin was a local language in Italy. As Rome became the leading Christian city, the Western rite moved out of Greek and into Latin. The Roman Church developed common texts in Latin, such as prayers for each Sunday and festival of the Church Year (Collects and Proper Prefaces). Standard Scripture readings were appointed (the lectionary) as well, and an unaccompanied style of music called plainsong developed that would be universal for a thousand years.

With only minor local variations, the rite of the Divine Service was pretty much the same throughout the West. The combined influence of the pope and the Holy Roman Emperor made this possible.

Of course, not all was rosy! Fixed in ancient Latin, the liturgy was eventually understood only by scholars. The priests hurriedly muttered their parts, while the choir sang most of the canticles and hymns alone. The common people felt cut off from the service. They began to express their piety mostly outside the service in community festivals and guilds.

Because priests were often poorly educated, sermons became rare, and there were theological problems that affected the liturgy. The Lord's Supper came to be viewed as a sacrifice offered by the people to God. Lay people began to receive only the bread (Christ's body), while only the priests took the chalice (Christ's blood). Sometimes the laity didn't commune at all, but merely adored consecrated bread on a side altar. And because of the new idea of purgatory, priests spent hours offering "private masses" for the sake of the dead. The liturgy was ripe for reform.

Reformation

Conservative Change

The Lutheran Reformation has been called "conservative." The Reformers wanted to "conserve" what was good about the Medieval Church, not throw it all out and start from scratch. This was how they approached the liturgy. They changed only what needed to be changed and kept what was good and wholesome.

In 1523, Luther provided guidelines for bishops to reform the traditional Latin Mass in their territory.

NEED TO KNOW

Mass is a traditional term for the Divine Service with Holy Communion. It probably comes from the words of "dismissal" at the end of the service. Lutherans continued to use the term for hundreds of years after the Reformation, though it is less common today.

It may surprise us that he wanted to keep the rite mostly in Latin . . . for the sake of the children! After all, Latin was at the heart of their education. But he wanted the Scripture readings, a sermon, and some hymns in German.

Three years later, Luther prepared a fully German order of service. Instead of just translating the Latin canticles (such as the Sanctus) into German, he used newly written hymns based on the canticles (e.g., *LSB* 960). This "German Mass" was popular in village churches without good schools. For hundreds of years, the Latin and German orders were used side by side among Lutherans. Our services today take the best from both traditions—in English, of course!

According to the Gospel

But how did Luther reform the rite? He wrote in the introduction to his Latin Mass:

> It is not now nor ever has been our intention to abolish the liturgical service of God completely, but rather to purify the one that is now in use from the wretched accretions which corrupt it and to point out an evangelical [Gospel] use. (AE 53:20)

Luther decided what was a "wretched accretion" by holding up the Gospel—justification by grace through faith on account of Christ alone—as a bright light to examine the Western rite. The most significant corruptions that he wanted to remove were the following:

- Scripture readings in Latin, which the people couldn't understand;
- the lack of preaching;
- the priest's *silent* praying of the Words of Institution;
- the sacrifice of the Mass; and
- Communion in one kind.

The most significant change, therefore, came at the point of the Lord's Supper. He

TECHNICAL STUFF

The "sacrifice of the Mass" refers to a medieval Roman Catholic teaching that Christ's body and blood were to be offered *to* God to make satisfaction for our sins. Luther argued on the basis of Jesus' own words ("for you") that Christ's body and blood were to be received as a gift *from* God.

WHAT DOES THIS MEAN?

Let us, therefore, repudiate everything that smacks of sacrifice, together with the entire canon and retain only that which is pure and holy, and so order our mass. (AE 53:26)

completely removed the offertory prayers and the priest's prayer, called the "canon of the Mass." He called these prayers a "sewer and cesspool" (AE 53:21), because they turned the Sacrament into a sacrifice. He replaced them with a sung proclamation of Christ's Words of Institution at the conclusion of the Preface.

Luther kept nearly everything else from the traditional Western rite. He believed that the classic songs of the liturgy such as the Agnus Dei beautifully proclaimed the Gospel. He wanted the people to hear the Scriptures and sing hymns in their own language. But, otherwise, he kept the normal rite and ceremonies, with comments on how the Gospel could be more clearly taught.*

BELIEVE, TEACH, CONFESS

The laity are given both kinds in the Sacrament of the Lord's Supper because this practice has the Lord's command, "Drink of it, all of you" (Matthew 26:27). Christ has clearly commanded that all should drink from the cup. (AC XXII 1–2)

From Then to Now

Decline . . .

Until the nineteenth century, Germany wasn't a unified country but a collection of territories and free cities. Early Lutherans were united by a common confession, but each territorial church had its own "church order." This included how the

NEED TO KNOW

Following the teachings of John Calvin, Calvinists speak of a "real presence" in Holy Communion, but they believe that communicants ascend to heaven by faith to meet Christ there. They deny that the bread and wine on the altar and in the mouth are Christ's body and blood, as Lutherans confess.

---

* Our churches are falsely accused of abolishing the Mass. The Mass is held among us and celebrated with the highest reverence. Nearly all the usual ceremonies are also preserved, except that the parts sung in Latin are interspersed here and there with German hymns. These have been added to teach the people. For ceremonies are needed for this reason alone, that the uneducated be taught ‹what they need to know about Christ›. Not only has Paul commanded that a language understood by the people be used in church (1 Corinthians 14:2, 9), but human law has also commanded it. All those able to do so partake of the Sacrament together. This also increases the reverence and devotion of public worship. No one is admitted to the Sacrament without first being examined. The people are also advised about the dignity and use of the Sacrament, about how it brings great consolation to anxious consciences, so that they too may learn to believe God and to expect and ask from Him all that is good. This worship pleases God [Colossians 1:9–10]. Such use of the Sacrament nourishes true devotion toward God. Therefore, it does not appear that the Mass is more devoutly celebrated among our adversaries than among us. (AC XXIV 1–9)

LUTHER'S LATIN RITE (1523) in Latin unless specified	LUTHER'S GERMAN RITE (1526) entirely in German
(Sermon in German)	
Introit or Psalm	Hymn or Psalm
Kyrie (ninefold)	Kyrie (threefold)
Gloria in Excelsis	[Gloria in Excelsis Hymn?]
Collect of the Day	Collect of the Day
Epistle (in German)	Epistle
Gradual and Hallelujah	
Hymn (in German)	Hymn
Gospel (in German)	Gospel
Nicene Creed	Nicene Creed Hymn (*LSB* 954)
(Sermon in German)	Sermon
Preparation of Bread and Wine	Paraphrase of the Lord's Prayer
Preface (Dialogue and Proper Prefaces)	Admonition to Communicants
Words of Institution	Consecration of the Bread
Sanctus	Distribution of the Consecrated Bread
Hymn (in German)	Sanctus hymn (*LSB* 960) or Other Hymn
Lord's Prayer	Consecration of the Cup
Pax Domini ("Peace")	Distribution of the Consecrated Cup
Agnus Dei and Distribution of Both Kinds	Agnus Dei or Other Hymn
Hymn (in German)	
Post-Communion: Collect Benedicamus Aaronic Benediction	Post-Communion: Collect Aaronic Benediction

liturgy was to be conducted. These orders mostly followed Luther's Latin or German rites, but there were minor differences from place to place.

In the early seventeenth century, Lutheranism was profoundly disrupted by the Thirty Years' War. At the end of the war, the Peace of Westphalia (1648) introduced a form of religious freedom that allowed the prince of each territory to choose its religion. In some places where nearly everyone was Lutheran, the prince nevertheless declared Calvinism to be the territorial faith. This had disastrous results for the Lutheran rite of Holy Communion in those places.

The war also had a profound effect on the ceremony of the liturgy. Church buildings and their furnishings were destroyed, precious Communion vessels were stolen, and pastors were killed. This had two consequences: (1) many Lutherans lost the habit of having Communion on every Sunday and festival; and (2) a generation got used to an extremely bare form of service.

In the seventeenth and eighteenth centuries, Lutheranism was troubled by two movements that did further damage to their liturgical life. "Pietism" emphasized personal devotion and had little respect for the public liturgy. "Rationalism" denied the power of the Word and the Sacraments entirely.

The immigrants who founded The Lutheran Church—Missouri Synod left Germany in 1838–39 to escape this un-Lutheran liturgical environment.

. . . and Recovery

The Missouri Synod's first president, C. F. W. Walther, reached behind Rationalism, Pietism, and the War to recover the faithful Lutheran church order of early Saxony. He published a German order of service for the Missouri Synod in 1856. He also published a hymnal (1847) that recovered the great hymns of early Lutheranism.

Walther's service was much more like Luther's German Mass than our services today. For example, the Confession and Absolution weren't at the beginning but were after the sermon. And he used hymns in place of some canticles, such as "All Glory Be to God on High" (*LSB* 947) for the Gloria in Excelsis.

Meanwhile, three other American Lutheran church bodies were getting together to produce a common order in English. In 1888, they published their "Common Service," based on "the common consent of the pure Lutheran liturgies of the sixteenth century." They took the English translations of the canticles, creeds, and prayers from Thomas Cranmer's work in the Anglican *Book of Common Prayer*—closing a circle begun when Cranmer first borrowed from Lutherans in 1549.

Missouri's English Hymnals

The Common Service was also included in the *Evangelical Lutheran Hymn Book*

(1889), published by the forerunner of the English District. This English-speaking synod donated their hymnal to the Missouri Synod when they joined in 1911. After a revised version was published in 1912, this hymnal was reworked to produce *The Lutheran Hymnal* in 1941. *TLH* included the Common Service as the beloved "page 15" Order of Holy Communion. It also introduced an order of morning service without Communion (p. 5).

The Missouri Synod began almost immediately to work on a new hymnal. In 1969, they published the *Worship Supplement* with new orders of service and nearly one hundred new hymns. They invited other synods into the Inter-Lutheran Commission on Worship with the goal of one hymnal for all American Lutherans. The result was *Lutheran Book of Worship* (1978).

This was a time when the LCMS was struggling with liberal theology, particularly in her seminaries. A synodical taskforce raised theological concerns about some parts of *LBW*. The new hymnal had also abandoned many orders and hymns that were dear to LCMS churches. Thus, in 1982, the LCMS published their own revision of *LBW* as *Lutheran Worship*.

The new hymnal had a mixed reception. While more than half of LCMS churches adopted it, many people thought the music was too difficult and that it had subtly changed well-known words and music. The Commission on Worship began work toward a new hymnal in 1996, hinting at what was to come in *Hymnal Supplement 98*.

After a decade of work and extensive field testing in congregations, *Lutheran Service Book* was published in 2006. By including the best of each hymnal, the goal was to encourage churches that used either *TLH* or *LW* to adopt the new book. While there are some new rites and more than one hundred new hymns, the musical settings have mostly returned to simpler four-part harmony, and the familiar language of many hymns has been restored. The five settings of the Divine Service are minor revisions of orders from both hymnals.

Study Questions

1. Which elements of our Divine Service were already present in the Early Apostolic Church, as we read in the New Testament?

2. What does "the breaking of the bread" mean in the New Testament and Early Church?

3. Why did early Christians meet on Sunday evening for the liturgy?

4. How did the conversion of Emperor Constantine affect Christian worship?

5. What changes did Luther bring to the medieval Mass?

Visit lutheranism101.com to download the free Leader's Guide.

Discussion Questions

1. Read the events of Easter evening from Luke 24:28–43. Discuss how Jesus sets the pattern for Christian worship immediately after His resurrection.

2. Discuss the changes that came to the liturgy in the Middle Ages. In what way were they both good and bad? What sort of problems in the liturgy cried out for reform?

3. Why is it significant that Luther didn't throw out the entire Roman rite of the liturgy but merely purged it of abuses and corruptions? What was his principle for reform?

4. Look through the setting of the Divine Service from *LSB* that is used most frequently in your church and compare it to the outline of Luther's Latin and German rites on page 72. In what ways is it the same or different?

5. If you have used older Lutheran hymnals like *TLH* or *LW*, or even hymnals from another church body, discuss how *LSB* responded to the challenge of providing liturgical resources for twenty-first-century English-speaking Lutherans.

CHAPTER 5

A Bird's-Eye View of the Divine Service

In This Chapter

- Seeing the big picture: understanding the outline, major parts, and flow of the Divine Service

Before setting out on a journey, it's important to look at a map. It's not enough to know just your final destination; you also need to be familiar with the landmarks along the route that help you to know you're on the right track. And often the journey itself is just as important as the journey's end. Each waypoint may be the place for a meal or fuel that keeps you going; or it may have a scenic lookout or attraction that makes the trip worthwhile.

Soon we will look at the various parts of the liturgy; but the liturgy is more than just an accumulation of things. You can walk the aisles of a supermarket in pretty much any order you want and fill your shopping cart. But the liturgy is a different kind of journey. It delivers God's gifts in a certain order, aiming for critical moments along the route and then arriving at a goal. And the liturgical traveler comes away not with a bag full of souvenirs but with a changed heart.

Remembering the Story of Salvation

When God instituted the Passover for His people Israel, He called it a "memorial day" (Exodus 12:14). By reenacting the meal of bitter herbs, unleavened bread, and roast lamb, the Israelites were to remember how God redeemed their forefathers from Egyptian slavery. The youngest child was to ask his father to explain the feast by retelling the story of the exodus.

We have seen that all the major feasts of the Old Testament were remembrances of God's saving deeds in history. The Israelites were not just to "remember" these events by thinking about them; they were also to tell the stories and carry out rites that made these ancient acts of salvation *their* salvation.

So, also, when Jesus transformed the Passover into the Lord's Supper and said, "Do this in remembrance of Me," He didn't mean simply that we should think about Him when we eat bread and drink wine. But in the Lord's Supper, we truly eat His flesh, given for us, and drink His blood, shed for us on the cross for the forgiveness of our sins. In His Supper, we celebrate His death and resurrection until He comes again in glory.

This miraculous "remembrance" of ancient deeds is made possible through God's mighty Word. In the Divine Service, God's Word proclaims and reenacts everything Jesus did for us. In certain places, this is explicit: the Creed and the Proper Prefaces, for example, tell the story plainly. The lectionary readings and the seasons of the Church Year take us through Christ's life step by step.

WHAT DOES THIS MEAN?

The first and foremost of all on which everything else depends, is the teaching of the Word of God. For we teach with the Word, we consecrate with the Word, we bind and absolve sins by the Word, we baptize with the Word, we sacrifice with the Word, we judge all things by the Word. (AE 40:21)

But as the Divine Service takes us from Jesus' teaching and preaching to the Supper He instituted on the night of His crucifixion, it also takes us through His life every Sunday. We sing the Christmas song of the angels in the Gloria in Excelsis and join the crowds on Palm Sunday singing, "Blessed is He who comes in the name of the Lord." The Divine Service is the story of salvation in miniature.

Beginning from Baptism

The liturgy begins with an entrance rite that recalls our personal story of salvation. It returns us to our Baptism by repeating the triune name and leading us to confess our sins and be forgiven. This entrance rite teaches us who we are and shows us how God calls us into His house.

But Baptism isn't just the beginning of our personal salvation story. Jesus' ministry began with His Baptism (Mark 1:1–11; Acts 10:37–38). There He took upon Himself the sins of the world and began to carry them to the cross. There He was anointed with the Holy Spirit for His messianic office. So, the departure point of the Divine Service is both our beginning and Christ's. We recall how Christ was baptized for us so that our sins could be placed on Him and washed away.

WHAT DOES THIS MEAN?

For among Christians the whole service should center in the Word and sacrament. (AE 53:90)

BELIEVE, TEACH, CONFESS

The Church is the assembly of saints in which the Gospel is purely taught and the Sacraments are correctly administered. (AC VII 1, author's translation)

WHAT DOES THIS MEAN?

Properly speaking, the mass consists in using the Gospel and communing at the table of the Lord. (AE 53:25)

Two Great Gifts

The Divine Service is built around the two great gifts that Christ bestowed on the Church: His proclaimed Word and His Supper. We saw that the apostles followed this pattern of worship immediately after Jesus' ascension, devoting themselves to His teaching and the breaking of bread, with prayer (Acts 2:42).

The nineteenth-century Lutheran pastor Wilhelm Loehe described the Divine Service as a mountain range dominated by two high peaks. We might think of Word and Sacrament as these two peaks. But "the Word" isn't just one part of the Divine Service; it is the driving force in every part, like a powerful river coursing through the mountains. Loehe pictured the sermon in particular as the first of the two peaks. Or we might see the reading of the Holy Gospel as that first peak, with the sermon flowing from it. Loehe saw the Lord's Supper as the second (and slightly higher) peak, the closest one can get to heaven's heights in this life.

In the journey of the Divine Service, these two peaks are the major waypoints. The rest of the order of service is designed to lead us to and from them, surrounding them with signposts to keep us focused on our destinations. In *LSB*, the major sections of the Divine Service are marked with headings:

CONFESSION AND ABSOLUTION
SERVICE OF THE WORD
SERVICE OF THE SACRAMENT

The first section isn't really a separate part but includes those things that we do to prepare for the service. It's a "Preparation Rite." We might also call it the "Entrance Rite," since most of the service before the Scripture readings was done historically while the clergy and choir processed to their places.

Ordinary and Propers

There are five main texts that all forms of the Western rite have in common. Originally they were sung by the choir, but in Lutheran churches today, they are usually sung or spoken by the congregation: Kyrie Eleison, Gloria in Excelsis, Nicene Creed, Sanctus, and Agnus Dei. We call these texts the "Ordinary" because they are almost always used. We might think of the Ordinary as the *skeleton* of the Divine Service, what gives it a sturdy shape.

Of course, those five ordinary texts aren't the only parts that stay the same each week. There are also responses between pastor and people such as the Salutation and Preface. And there are crucial biblical texts, including the Lord's Prayer, Words of Institution, and Benediction.

The parts of the service that do change each week or season are called "Propers," because they are "proper" to the day. They include the Introit, Collect of the Day, Scripture readings, Gradual, and so on. Think of the Propers as the *flesh* on the skeleton, giving it vitality, movement, and growth.

MAKING CONNECTIONS

The Western rite of the liturgy is common among Lutherans, Roman Catholics, and Anglicans and looks very much alike in those churches. There are some differences in rite and ceremony that simply reflect natural human diversity. Other differences arise from the distinct doctrinal teachings of each church.

Finally, there are parts of the Divine Service that have become normal for English-speaking Lutherans. For example, there's a public Confession and Absolution at the beginning of all five settings in *LSB*, but this isn't done in all Lutheran or other Western churches. We might think of these normal additions as the *clothing* that gives the service a distinct character.

Sacramental and Sacrificial Rhythm

We have learned that Lutherans use the terms *sacramental* and *sacrificial* to distinguish (1) the parts of the service in which God serves us with His Gospel gifts from (2) those in which we respond with prayer, praise, and thanksgiving. In true Christian worship, God's gifts should predominate over our feeble response.

The Lutheran Divine Service has a particularly well-tuned balance between the two. This comes fundamentally from building the service around those two great gifts of Word and Supper. The service then provides appropriate ways for us to respond to the gifts.

It's vital not only to keep the balance right but also to keep the order right. Wouldn't it be absurd to proclaim the forgiveness of sins before we speak our confession? It works the other way around. So, also, God speaks to us in the Scripture readings before we respond to Him by confessing the Creed, which is taken from those Scriptures. We proclaim the promises of God in Scripture and sermon before we take up those promises and beg for His help in the Prayer of the

The Divine Service Outline

Ordinary "skeleton" — Choral	Ordinary "skeleton" — Pastoral	Propers "flesh"	Lutheran Additions "clothing"
Preparation Rite			
			Hymn of Invocation
			Invocation
			Versicles
			Confession and Absolution
I. Service of the Word			
1. Kyrie		Introit	
2. Gloria in Excelsis			
	Salutation		
		Collect of the Day	
		Old Testament	
		Gradual	
	Alleluia	Epistle	
	Ascriptions of Praise	Verse	
3. Nicene Creed		Gospel	
		Hymn of the Day	
		Sermon	
		Bridge:	Prayer of the Church
			Offering
			Offertory
II. Service of the Sacrament			
	Preface Dialogue		
		Proper Preface	
4. Sanctus			Distribution Hymns
	Our Father		Nunc Dimittis
	Words of Our Lord		
	Pax Domini		
5. Agnus Dei			
	Post-Communion Collect		
	Benedicamus		Benediction

The Divine Service as Sacrament and Sacrifice

God

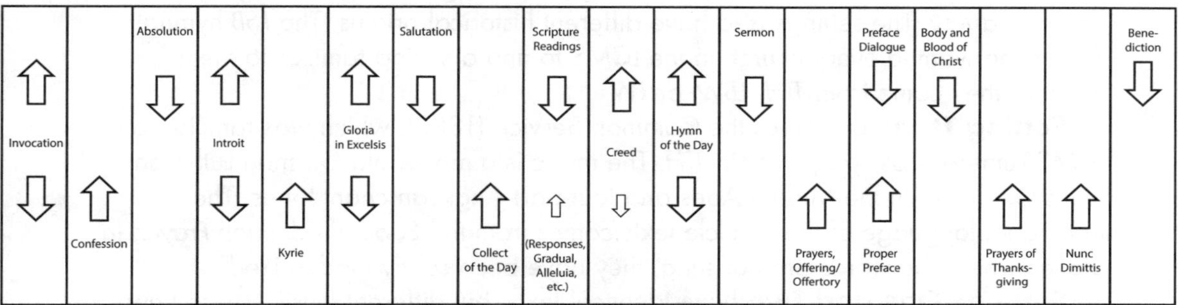

The Christian

Church. And we pray our thanks and say our Amen chiefly after we have received the Lord's precious body and blood.

The careful rhythmic heartbeat of the Lutheran Divine Service saves us from the sort of me-centered worship that we might otherwise invent if left to ourselves. Whenever we're tempted to say, "Look what I can do for You, God!" the Divine Service trumps our selfish claims with His overwhelmingly gracious gifts.

Nothing but Scripture

One more thing: God not only comes to us first in worship, but He also actually gives us the words to say when we respond. God teaches us to worship Him the way a father teaches a child to speak. He patiently repeats a word and then waits for his young child to mouth the same word back. And when he hears "Dadda" for the first time, a father's face beams with joy!

MAKING CONNECTIONS

Saying back to him what he has said to us, we repeat what is most true and sure. (*LW*, p. 6)

So, also, the Divine Service is nearly 100 percent Scripture. This has always been true, but it is highlighted in *LSB* by the inclusion of Scripture references next to nearly every part of the liturgy. We can know that our worship is pleasing to God if we use the very words He gives us.

Five Settings

LSB provides five settings of the Divine Service. Each setting is a version of the Western rite in Lutheran dress. The minor variations in the order of elements and texts, as well as the different musical settings, are designed to give congregations healthy variety. The settings also have different historical origins. The *LSB* hymnal committee wanted every church in the LCMS to find a setting familiar to them, whether they came from *TLH*, *LBW*, or *LW*.

Setting Three preserves the Common Service (1888), which was familiar to LCMS Lutherans as "page 15" in *TLH*. The music is a mix of old German Lutheran tunes with roots in the Middle Ages and four-part Anglican chant tones. The traditional language of the canticle texts comes from the *Book of Common Prayer*. In places where the words are not sung, they have been subtly modernized.

Settings One and Two have identical texts, but different music. These new versions of the Lutheran rite were prepared in the 1960s for use in a new hymnal. The settings include new canticles ("This Is the Feast," "Thank the Lord") and an expanded version of the Kyrie. The modern translations of the canticles come from an ecumenical committee.

Setting Five is based on Luther's German Mass (1526), using classic Lutheran hymns in place of the canticles. The order of service is filled out so that it more closely resembles the other settings in *LSB*.

Setting Four is a simpler setting of the service, originally prepared for *Hymnal Supplement 98*. Following the example of Luther's German Mass, it uses hymns in place of the canticles, though these are more modern hymns. As in Setting Five, there is no chant music provided for dialogue between pastor and people.

Study Questions

1. What are the two major parts of the Divine Service? Within the two parts, what are the central elements?

2. What do we mean by the distinction between "Ordinary" and "Propers" in the liturgy?

Discussion Questions

1. Discuss how the use of Ordinary and Propers in careful balance can give the liturgy both consistency and variety. What can go wrong when the liturgy has too much or too little change?

2. Using the Scripture references next to each part of the liturgy in *LSB*, note how much of your usual setting of the Divine Service is taken straight from Scripture. Discuss the accusation we sometimes hear that the liturgy is "just man-made."

CHAPTER 6

The Divine Service: The Path on the Ground

In This Chapter

- The details: learning the biblical roots and historical growth of the service's parts
- The focus: seeing the Gospel proclamation of Christ throughout

Preparation Rite

Invocation

The first words of the liturgy are the name of the triune God that was put on us at our Baptism. Although we call these words the **Invocation**, we don't say these words to conjure up an absent God. God is already present. But He is pleased to hear us remember our Baptism and acknowledge Him as our Father as we enter His house.

As this is a remembrance of Baptism, it's appropriate for God's people to join with their pastor in making the sign of the cross that was first put on them at the font. Historically, these words were part of the priest's private devotions before the service and were also said silently by each worshiper who entered the church. The Invocation is a private devotional act made public.

FROM THE BIBLE

Go therefore and make disciples of all nations, baptizing them in the name of the Father and of the Son and of the Holy Spirit, teaching them to observe all that I have commanded you. And behold, I am with you always, to the end of the age. (Matthew 28:19–20)

Where God's name is spoken, we can be confident that He is in our midst with all His gifts. In the Old Testament, God promised to bless His people wherever He caused His name to dwell (Exodus 20:24). In the New Testament, Jesus attaches the same promise to His name. The Invocation reminds us that through Christ's name, we have access to the Father's throne by the Spirit (Ephesians 2:18).

Confession and Absolution

The church is a forgiveness house where repentant sinners come to be freed from their sins (Matthew 18:15–20). Although it has somewhat fallen out of practice among modern Lutherans, Individual Confession and Absolution (*LSB*, p. 292) with a pastor in private is the usual way to confess and receive forgiveness (John 20:22–23).

The general **Confession and Absolution** in the Divine Service is not meant to replace private confession. Like the Invocation, it comes from a private rite of preparation that the priest and his assistants would do before the service. In the Middle Ages and early Lutheranism, it sometimes became a public rite, as it is in all five settings in *LSB*.

We might compare confession and absolution to Moses' taking off his shoes before drawing near to the Lord in the burning bush (Exodus 3:5). We confess that our sins have made us dirty and that we need to be cleansed before entering the Lord's holy house. This confession is a return to the cleansing waters of our Baptism (Hebrews 10:22).

We are driven to confession by God's Word, which uncovers our sins and promises God's forgiveness. So we hear God speak first with responsive words from Scripture before we confess.

Service of the Word

The Divine Service is divided into two main parts, the Service of the Word and the Service of the Sacrament. We'll first look at the details of the Service of the Word. While the main features of the Service of the Word are the reading of Scripture and the sermon, there are many parts to the service.

NEED TO KNOW

Invocation comes from the Latin for "call upon" and refers to speaking the name of our triune God at the beginning of a service.

MAKING CONNECTIONS

Most true and sure is his name, which he put upon us with the water of our Baptism. We are his. This we acknowledge at the beginning of the Divine Service. Where his name is, there is he. (*LW*, p. 6)

FROM THE BIBLE

For where two or three are gathered in My name, there am I among them. (Matthew 18:20)

Introit, Psalm, or Entrance Hymn

Why Sing Psalms?

The Psalms are the hymnal of the Old Testament. Jesus, as the Son of David, claims them as His own. The Psalms prophesy about Him (Luke 24:44), and Jesus takes them up as His own prayers, most poignantly when He quotes Psalm 22 from the cross (Matthew 27:46). Thus, it's fitting that Christian worship be filled with the Psalms, since Jesus is leading our worship of the Father. Paul encourages us to sing "psalms and hymns and songs of the Spirit" (Ephesians 5:19, author's translation).

Psalms appear throughout the Divine Service: in the Confession and Absolution, the Introit, the Psalm or Gradual between the readings, and the Offertory. By using the Psalms, we offer praise to God with His own words and in unity with all Christians.

Introit

The **Introit** arose in the fifth century when churches became larger and the ceremony of the liturgy more elaborate. The choir sang psalms as the minister and his assistants processed to their places. In the Middle Ages, the Introit was shortened to just a few verses, chosen to praise God according to the particular season of the Church Year.

Introits follow a standard pattern, which is simply the way all psalms were traditionally sung:

- Antiphon
- Psalm Verses
- Gloria Patri
- Antiphon

Because the Psalms were meant to be sung, *LSB* provides simple musical tones for the choir or congregation to sing the Introit. The Introit may be replaced with a full **Psalm** or an **Entrance Hymn**. The pastor (and assistants) may process into the chancel during this song.

MAKING CONNECTIONS

We can see some variety in the opening moves of the Divine Service. Sometimes a pastor may use the rite of Corporate Confession and Absolution (*LSB*, p. 290), in which the congregation comes to the altar rail to be absolved one by one. This expanded rite, which includes a mini sermon (Confessional Address), often took place on Saturday night or on Sunday at a time before the service. When a Baptism is part of the Divine Service, it often takes place at the beginning of the service. In this case, the Confession and Absolution might be omitted, because watching the Baptism reminds us of our own Baptism in a similar way.

NEED TO KNOW

In Latin, the word *Introit* (inn-TRO-it) means "he enters." It refers to the processional entrance of the minister with his assistants.

FROM THE BIBLE

Enter His gates with thanksgiving, and His courts with praise! Give thanks to Him; bless His name! (Psalm 100:4)

NEED TO KNOW

The word *antiphon* comes from Greek and means "responsive sound." An antiphon is a thematic verse repeated before and after a psalm or canticle.

NEED TO KNOW

Gloria Patri in Latin means "glory to the Father." The title comes from the first words: "*Glory be to the Father* and to the Son and to the Holy Spirit; as it was in the beginning, is now, and will be forever. Amen."

Gloria Patri

The **Gloria Patri** is an ancient form of praise that confesses the divinity of all three persons of the Trinity. In the fourth century, the Church encouraged its use to combat the heresy of Arianism, which denied that Jesus is true God.

But more positively, we sing this doxology because all true worship must be trinitarian: to the Father through the Son in the Holy Spirit. We add the Gloria Patri to psalms to confess that the God of the Old Testament was the triune God.

Kyrie ~ *Lord, Have Mercy*

The **Kyrie** is a cry to God for mercy and help. In the Old Testament, God showed Himself to Israel as a merciful God, and so they cried to Him for help in temple worship (Psalm 6:2 KJV). In the Gospels, Jesus has mercy on all sorts of sick, blind, and lame beggars who seek His help.

Although penitent sinners cry to a merciful God for forgiveness (Luke 18:13), the Kyrie is more a cry for help in *all* our needs, earthly and heavenly (Hebrews 4:16).

NEED TO KNOW

In Greek, *Kyrie Eleison* (KIH-ree-ay ee-LEH-ee-son) means "Lord, have mercy!" It can be prayed on its own or spoken as a response to petitions.

When it came into the liturgy in the fifth century, it was as a response to a series of petitions in a litany. The Eastern Orthodox still have a Kyrie litany at the beginning of their Divine Service. We have a short version of it in *LSB*, Settings One and Two. Notice how these petitions cover every human need.

The Western Church eventually kept just the threefold cry, "Lord, have mercy! Christ, have mercy! Lord, have mercy!" (*LSB*, Settings Three and Four). Although we might think of this as trinitarian, it's really addressed to Jesus, who is both Lord and Christ. We begin the service by admitting that we are little more than beggars in need of His help. We cry to Jesus as a King who is really present with us.

The Kyrie appears again within the Gloria in Excelsis, in the Agnus Dei, as a response in the Prayer of the Church, and also in the daily offices.

FROM THE BIBLE

And behold, there were two blind men sitting by the road-side, and when they heard that Jesus was passing by, they cried out, "Lord, have mercy on us, Son of David!" The crowd rebuked them, telling them to be silent, but they cried out all the more, "Lord, have mercy on us, Son of David!" (Matthew 20:30–31)

Hymn of Praise–Gloria in Excelsis ~ *Glory to God in the Highest*

Later in the service, the pastor will say that we praise God "with angels and archangels and with all the company of heaven" (Preface). We then sing the Sanctus, because it is the angels' own song. The **Gloria in Excelsis** is introduced with another song of the angels, from Christmas Eve (Luke 2:14). From beginning to end, we confess that the Divine Service is part of the worship of heaven. We sing this Christmas song to confess that Jesus comes to us in the flesh, just as the disciples confessed when they repeated the song on Palm Sunday (Luke 19:38).

After that angelic introduction—sung by the pastor as an antiphon—the ancient hymn itself begins. The Gloria was known already in the fourth century and began as a special hymn of praise for Christmas Eve. By the eleventh century,

NEED TO KNOW

A "litany" is an ancient form of extended prayer in which the leader speaks a petition and the people voice their agreement with a brief, repeated response. See *LSB*, p. 288, for the Great Litany.

NEED TO KNOW

Gloria in Excelsis (GLORY-a in ex-CHEL-sis) is Latin for "glory in the highest," the opening words of this hymn of praise.

FROM THE BIBLE

Glory to God in the highest, and on earth peace among those with whom He is pleased! (Luke 2:14)

WHAT DOES THIS MEAN?

The good news was preached and sung for us by angels, who are heavenly theologians and have rejoiced in our behalf! Their song is the most glorious. It contains the whole Christian faith. For the *gloria in excelsis* is supreme worship. They wish us such worship and they bring it to us in Christ. (AE 54:327)

it was used in every service—except for Advent and Lent, when it is omitted to emphasize the penitential mood that characterizes those seasons.

The hymn is trinitarian, but it centers on Jesus. After glorifying God the Father, it proclaims Jesus as God's Son and the Lamb who takes away our sins (John 1:29). True praise declares God's saving deeds. What it says about Jesus sounds very much like the Creed. It ends with Jesus at the right hand of God to receive our praise with the Father and the Holy Spirit.

This Is the Feast

LSB Settings One and Two provide a hymn of praise written in the 1960s for a new setting of the Divine Service. The text draws on the angelic songs sung in John's vision of heaven (e.g., Revelation 5:9–14).

The antiphon, "This is the feast of victory for our God," reminds us that in the Divine Service, we are joined to the wedding banquet in heaven (Isaiah 25:6; Revelation 19:9). The song celebrates Christ's resurrection and points ahead to the Lord's Supper. This hymn of praise is particularly appropriate for the Easter season.

Salutation

St. Augustine tells us that in his day (fourth century), the Divine Service began with an apostolic greeting from the priest (e.g., 2 Corinthians 13:14) and that the Scripture readings immediately followed. The **Salutation** recalls that ancient beginning of the service.

When the angel Gabriel appeared to Mary, saying, "The Lord is with you" (Luke 1:28), it was more than a wish. For with these words, Jesus became flesh in Mary's womb. When the pastor says, "The Lord be with you" (2 Thessalonians 3:16), we know that Jesus is really coming to us in the Scripture readings and the Lord's Supper.

The congregation responds "and with thy spirit" to recognize that the pastor received the Holy Spirit in ordination to empower his work (2 Timothy 4:22). In other settings in *LSB*, the congregation returns his heartfelt greeting, saying, "And also with you." This regular greeting in the liturgy affirms and strengthens the loving relationship between pastor and people.

FROM THE BIBLE

I heard around the throne . . . the voice of many angels, numbering myriads of myriads and thousands of thousands, saying with a loud voice, "Worthy is the Lamb who was slain, to receive power and wealth and wisdom and might and honor and glory and blessing!" (Revelation 5:11–12)

Collect of the Day

The pastor prepares our hearts to hear God's Word by praying the **Collect of the Day**. Saying "Let us pray," he gives the congregation a moment to think, then "collects" their needs and prays for them as Jesus' representative. The Collect is a "proper" that expresses the theme of the readings, festival, or season.

The Collect follows a pattern than can instruct us in our prayers. It generally includes these five parts:

1. Address: "O God . . ."
2. Rationale: "because You are . . ."
3. Petition: "grant that we . . ."
4. Benefit: "so that . . ."
5. Doxology: "through Jesus Christ . . ."

The Collect appeals to the gracious nature and promises of God before asking Him for help. The concluding doxology teaches us that we pray to the Father through the Son. And it reminds us that prayer includes praise as well as petition (Ephesians 3:14–21). The congregation says a firm "Amen" to voice their agreement with the prayer.

NEED TO KNOW

Salutation comes from the Latin word for "greeting." It refers to an intimate dialogue between pastor, *"The Lord be with you,"* and people, *"and with your spirit."*

Readings

God commanded His Old Testament people to read aloud the Books of Moses in their worship (Deuteronomy 31:11; see also Exodus 24:7; Joshua 8:34–35; Nehemiah 8–9). In the synagogue, the Jews read from the Pentateuch and the Prophets according to a lectionary system (Acts 13:15). St. Paul urged the churches to which he wrote

MAKING CONNECTIONS

Here, the Collect for the Fifth Sunday of Easter is marked with the five parts: "(1) O God, (2) You make the minds of Your faithful to be of one will. (3) Grant that we may love what You have commanded and desire what You promise, (4) that among the many changes of this world our hearts may be fixed where true joys are found; (5) through Jesus Christ, Your Son, our Lord, who lives and reigns with You and the Holy Spirit, one God, now and forever." (*LSB Altar Book*)

NEED TO KNOW

Amen is a Hebrew word meaning "it is true." It is a congregational response by which they affirm the pastor's prayer as their own (1 Corinthians 14:16). It is also added to doxologies to say, "I believe it!"

to read his epistles aloud during the Divine Service (Colossians 4:16). John also assumed his Revelation would be read by a lector to a gathered congregation (Revelation 1:3).

Paul tells Timothy that the public reading of Scripture is a vital part of the pastoral ministry, together with preaching and teaching (1 Timothy 4:13). Through the reading of these inspired writings, the Holy Spirit condemns sin, creates faith, and delivers Jesus to the hearers.

The **Readings** follow a lectionary that gives three readings appropriate to the Sunday or festival (see ch. 7). The appointed readings form the basis of the pastor's sermon.

The Holy Gospel is the most important of the three because it gives the very words of Jesus and sets the theme of the day. Jesus stands in our midst and speaks to us (John 20:19)! For this reason, it is adorned with special ceremonies: we sing **Alleluia** and words of praise to Jesus, and we stand for its reading. The pastor may also process into the midst of the congregation to read the Gospel, symbolizing the coming of Christ.

Responses

The responses to the readings teach us what is happening and give us words to express our thanks and praise. The pastor says, "This is the Word of the Lord," and the people respond, "Thanks be to God." The Gradual provides seasonal words from a psalm in response to the First Reading—or a whole psalm may be used. The Verse is another portion of Scripture chosen according to the season to adorn the Holy Gospel. There is also a common verse in

NEED TO KNOW

Gradual comes from the Latin word for "step" because these words of praise from the Psalms were originally sung from the steps leading up to the place of reading.

Settings One, Two (John 6:68), and Four (20:31).

Creed

We respond to God's Word by confessing back to Him who He says He is (Matthew 16:13–17). The first Christian creed is "Jesus is Lord." The Holy Spirit through the Word inspires us to make this faithful confession and be saved (Romans 10:9; 1 Corinthians 12:3), for Jesus will then confess us before His Father (Matthew 10:32).

The **Apostles' Creed** began as the Old Roman Creed in the second century. It was used in the baptismal liturgy to express the triune faith. The **Nicene Creed** also began as a baptismal creed. It was adopted by the Councils of Nicaea (AD 325) and Constantinople (AD 381) to confess the true divinity of Jesus in the face of the Arian heresy, which (like Jehovah's Witnesses today) viewed Jesus as a semi-divine creature. This is why the Second Article is so much longer than the other two. Between the fifth and the tenth centuries, churches adopted the Nicene Creed into the Divine Service as they fought against such heresy.

When it takes its traditional Western place after the Gospel, the Creed is a response to the readings. In the Eastern tradition, congregations confess the Creed just before Holy Communion as an expression of the common faith held by those who commune together. *LSB* provides both locations.

The Apostles' Creed is normally said at Baptism and in daily prayer. But *LSB* provides it as an alternative in the Divine Service for non-festival seasons.

NEED TO KNOW

Creed is from the Latin *credo*, "I believe." A creed is a statement of the trinitarian Christian faith, drawn from the Scriptures and handed down through the Church.

FROM THE BIBLE

Blessed is the one who reads aloud the words of this prophecy, and blessed are those who hear, and who keep what is written in it, for the time is near. (Revelation 1:3)

FROM THE BIBLE

Until I come, devote yourself to the public reading of Scripture, to exhortation, to teaching. (1 Timothy 4:13)

BELIEVE, TEACH, CONFESS

And the usual public ceremonies are observed, the series of lessons, of prayers, vestments, and other such things. . . . Ceremonies should be celebrated to teach people Scripture, that those admonished by the Word may conceive faith and godly fear, and may also pray. (Ap XXIV 1, 3)

Speaking the Creed every Sunday keeps before our eyes the creating, redeeming, and sanctifying work of God. It is the "common faith" (Titus 1:4), a deposit entrusted into our hands for us to treasure (2 Timothy 1:14).

Hymn of the Day

We sing hymns at many points in the service, but this one is special. The **Hymn of the Day** is a "proper" appointed to fit the Gospel or theme of the day. Early Lutherans took the Latin hymns sung by the choir before the Gospel and turned them into congregational hymns.

There are three benefits to following the Hymn of the Day list. (1) These hymns reinforce the message of the Gospel and form the first "preaching" on it. (2) Churches that follow the list will learn the core hymns of Lutheranism (and other churches). When Lutherans move from church to church, they will be sure to know at least these hymns. (3) The choir will have access to hundreds of years of resources written to go with these great Christian hymns. These hymns, for example, were the basis of Bach's cantatas, which were sung at this point in the service.

Often the Hymn of the Day is quite long. The congregation may better ponder its deep words by alternating stanzas between men and women, left and right sides, choir and congregation, or even by contemplating the words silently while the instrumentalists play the music.

NEED TO KNOW

Alleluia is a Hebrew word meaning "Praise Yahweh" or "Praise the LORD." It appears throughout the Psalms as a call to worship and in Revelation 19:1–6 on the lips of the heavenly host.

MAKING CONNECTIONS

During Lent, the Alleluia is omitted to express the penitential character of the season. When it returns at Easter, it sounds all the more joyful. "Return to the Lord, your God" (Joel 2:13) is a Lenten alternative in Settings One and Two.

Sermon

We see in the Bible that whenever the Scriptures were read, someone provided teaching and application of that Word to the gathered people (Luke 4:16–21; Acts 13:15). When the pastor preaches on the Scriptures, he continues the preaching ministry of Jesus. Jesus gave His apostles a command to preach and promised that He would be present in their preaching (Matthew 28:19; Luke 24:47). Luther was adamant that preaching, which had disappeared from many churches in the Middle Ages, should be restored.

The **Sermon** leads the congregation from

the Scripture readings to the Lord's Supper. Good preaching takes one or more of the appointed readings as a "text" and interprets it for today. It applies the Word of Law and Gospel to the congregation, exposing their sin, delivering their Savior, and teaching them the ways of God. In this way, it prepares them to be worthy participants in the Sacrament of the Altar that follows.

Lutheran preachers traditionally begin with the blessing of grace and peace drawn from the opening of Paul's epistles. They close with the Votum, a blessing of peace that comes from hearing God's Word (Philippians 4:7). By beginning and ending with Paul's words, the preacher submits himself to apostolic teaching (Acts 2:42).

FROM THE BIBLE

But what does it say? "The word is near you, in your mouth and in your heart" (that is, the word of faith that we proclaim); because, if you confess with your mouth that Jesus is Lord and believe in your heart that God raised Him from the dead, you will be saved. (Romans 10:8–9)

Prayer of the Church

The Prayer of the Church, Offering, and Offertory come in slightly different order in the various settings in *LSB*. This is because they form a bridge section that connects the Service of the Word to the Service of the Sacrament and relate to both.

FROM THE BIBLE

Preach the word; be ready in season and out of season; reprove, rebuke, and exhort, with complete patience and teaching. (2 Timothy 4:2)

The **Prayer of the Church** can be understood as a response to the Scripture readings and sermon. Having heard the promises of God, we lay our needs before Him. But it also looks to the Lord's Supper, since Christ's body and blood nourish us in body and soul. In ancient times, the Prayer of the Church led right into the Eucharistic Prayer.

The Prayer of the Church is more than prayer for individual needs. We pray for the whole world, for peace and good government, for salvation for all, and for the Church throughout the world (1 Timothy 2:1–4). As the priesthood of the baptized, we intercede first for others, and then we pray for ourselves. So, we add to these general prayers the particular needs of our congregations.

True Christian prayer is trinitarian. Jesus has given us access to the Father's throne of grace. We use that access for the benefit of others by praying through His name to the Father by the Spirit's power (Ephesians 2:18).

WHAT DOES THIS MEAN?

Now in order to correct these abuses, know first of all that a Christian congregation should never gather together without the preaching of God's Word and prayer, no matter how briefly. (AE 53:11)

FROM THE BIBLE

Grace to you and peace from God our Father and the Lord Jesus Christ. (Ephesians 1:2)

FROM THE BIBLE

First be reconciled to your brother, and then come and offer your gift. (Matthew 5:24)

Offering and Offertory

An **offering** from the flock or the field was a vital part of thankful worship in the Old Testament, acknowledging that all good things come from God. The offerings also supported the priests, the Levites, and the poor (Deuteronomy 26:1–13).

Jesus approves offerings for the poor done with the right spirit (Matthew 6:1–4). But He insists that we be reconciled with our brothers before bringing our offerings (5:23–24). *LSB* Settings One and Two provide the opportunity to share the peace to express this reconciliation. Saying "peace be with you" is also meant to express the unity in the common faith that is necessary to commune together, expressed in ancient times by exchanging a "holy kiss" (1 Corinthians 16:20). This is the original location and meaning of the Pax Domini (the Peace).

In the Early Church, members would bring forward gifts of bread and wine during an "offertory procession." The pastor would take enough for the Lord's Supper and set aside the rest to support himself and care for the congregation's poor. Today, we tend to provide money in the offering plate for these needs. We are obligated to support the preachers of the Gospel (1 Corinthians 9:13–14). Our offerings join our prayer and praise as a spiritual sacrifice in response to hearing the Word (1 Peter 2:5).

The **Offertory** was originally a psalm text sung while the offerings were brought forward. In the Middle Ages, it degenerated into a prayer expressing the sacrifice of the Mass, and so Luther simply threw it out! Our services restore the use of psalms. "Create in Me" (Psalm 51; Setting Three, *LSB*, pp. 192–93) expresses the attitude of the penitential heart in response to the sermon. "What Shall I Render" (Psalm 116; Settings One and Two, *LSB*, pp. 159–60; 176) teaches us that God doesn't need our offerings, but that we thank Him best by taking up and drinking from the cup of salvation in the Lord's Supper.

Service of the Sacrament

Preface

The **Preface** dialogue with its three responsive pairs (versicles and responses) is one of the most ancient parts of the liturgy, going back at least to the second century when Hippolytus quoted it.

The first pair is a repeat of the Salutation: "The Lord be with you. And with thy spirit." It expresses again the intimate relationship between pastor and people. But it also confesses that the Lord Jesus *is* with us in His body and blood and through His minister. His name comes first because He Himself is presiding at the altar and serving us (Luke 22:27).

"Lift up your hearts" sounds like an encouragement to be joyful. But it's really a reminder to look beyond plain bread and wine to find the Sacrament's meaning. For in it the resurrected Jesus comes to us with heavenly gifts (Colossians 3:1–3).

Finally, the pastor says, "Let us give thanks to the Lord, our God." This reminds us that the Lord's Supper was called the "Eucharist," or "Thanksgiving," by the Early Church. Jesus prayed a prayer of thanksgiving, "blessing" (praising) God before He instituted the Sacrament (Matthew 26:27). Paul also speaks of giving thanks in his observance of the meal (1 Corinthians 10:30).

Following the Preface dialogue, the pastor prays a great prayer of thanksgiving called the **Proper Preface**. The pastor does what Christ did—better said, Christ acts through the pastor. As the beginning of the prayer states, it is right to give thanks at all times (2 Thessalonians 1:3). But at this point, the Proper Preface, which changes from season to season, gives thanks for the saving work of Christ at that particular time of the Church Year. These are ancient prayers going back to the fourth century.

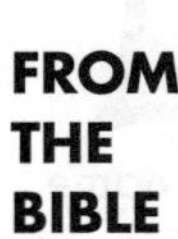

FROM THE BIBLE

Let the one who is taught the word share all good things with the one who teaches. (Galatians 6:6)

FROM THE BIBLE

What shall I render to the LORD for all His benefits to me? I will lift up the cup of salvation and call on the name of the LORD. (Psalm 116:12–13)

FROM THE BIBLE

If then you have been raised with Christ, seek the things that are above, where Christ is, seated at the right hand of God. Set your minds on things that are above, not on things that are on earth. For you have died, and your life is hidden with Christ in God. (Colossians 3:1–3)

NEED TO KNOW

Eucharist is an ancient name for the Lord's Supper that comes from the Greek word for thanksgiving. It refers to the prayer of thanksgiving that Jesus made before the meal, and to the presider's prayer of thanksgiving in the liturgy today.

TECHNICAL STUFF

The Proper Preface begins, "It is truly meet, right, and salutary . . ." "Meet" means "appropriate" and "salutary" means good for us in a "saving" way.

NEED TO KNOW

Sanctus means "holy" in Latin. The title comes from the first words of the angelic song from Isaiah 6:3.

Sanctus ~ *Holy, Holy, Holy*

The final words of the Proper Preface remind us that in the Divine Service, we stand together "with angels and archangels and with all the company of heaven." So it is quite appropriate to sing their song of praise!

The **Sanctus** is based on the song of the angelic seraphim that Isaiah saw flying around the throne of God in heaven (Isaiah 6:1–3). Isaiah received his vision while he was in the temple. God was showing him the heavenly worship that goes on invisibly during our earthly worship. The threefold "Holy, holy, holy" reminds us that the God of the Old Testament is our triune God. Jesus says that Isaiah saw *His* glory (John 12:41).

When John is granted a vision of heaven on the Lord's day, he also sees the angels singing "Holy, holy, holy" (Revelation 4:8). Again we learn that our worship is joined to the worship of heaven. For both "heaven and earth" are full of God's glory.

The second part of the Sanctus quotes the words of the crowds praising Jesus during His triumphant entry into Jerusalem on Palm Sunday: "Hosanna . . . Blessed is He who comes in the name of the Lord" (Matthew 21:9). The crowds were singing Psalm 118:25–26 and recognized that Jesus fulfilled it that day. We sing it in the liturgy to acknowledge that Jesus comes to us in His body and blood to bring us salvation.

The Jews sang the Sanctus in temple and synagogue worship. Its appearance in John's Revelation suggests Christians might have been singing it already in the first century. The Sanctus is surely one of the oldest and most profound parts of the liturgy.

Prayer of Thanksgiving

Settings One, Two, and Four include a **Prayer of Thanksgiving** after the Sanctus. This is really an extension of the Proper Preface, giving thanks to God specifically for the Lord's Supper. The opening words, "Blessed are You, Lord of heaven and earth," follow a traditional Jewish form of prayer found frequently in the Bible (Ephesians 1:3–14). In this context, "blessed" means "worthy of praise."

Lord's Prayer

Jesus taught the **Lord's Prayer** to His disciples (Matthew 6:9–13; Luke 11:2–4). He invited them to address God as He did and together with Him as "Our Father." Baptized children of God have this great privilege (Romans 8:14–17). The seven petitions are a comprehensive model for how we should pray. We know we will be heard when we use the prayer Jesus gave us. This prayer appears in virtually every rite of the Christian Church.

The **Doxology**, "For Thine is the kingdom . . . ," is not part of the prayer Jesus taught but is an early Christian liturgical response. These words of praise are based on David's prayer (1 Chronicles 29:11–13). The Doxology appeared in very early texts (e.g., *Didache*) and soon found its way even into copies of the Bible.

In Setting Three, we see the original pattern. The pastor, standing in the place of Jesus, prays the Our Father as a table prayer before the Lord's Supper, just as Jesus prayed on Holy Thursday before giving His Supper. The congregation voices their agreement and praises God with the Doxology and Amen. In the other settings, the pastor and congregation pray the whole prayer together as a family prayer. Many ancient Christians understood "Give us this day our daily bread, and forgive us our trespasses" as a reference to the Sacrament. Together with the Words of Our Lord, the Lord's Prayer is *consecratory*, setting aside the bread and wine for holy use (1 Timothy 4:4–5).

FROM THE BIBLE

In the year that King Uzziah died I saw the Lord sitting upon a throne, high and lifted up; and the train of His robe filled the temple. Above Him stood the seraphim. Each had six wings: with two he covered his face, and with two he covered his feet, and with two he flew. And one called to another and said: "Holy, holy, holy is the LORD of hosts; the whole earth is full of His glory!" (Isaiah 6:1–3)

TECHNICAL STUFF

The second part of the Sanctus is called the *Benedictus qui venit*, which is Latin for "Blessed is He who comes."

NEED TO KNOW

Hosanna is a Hebrew word of praise meaning "Save us now." We sing it to Jesus just as the Palm Sunday crowds did.

WHAT DOES THIS MEAN?

I believe that many hymns were included and retained in the mass which deal with thanking and praising [God] in a wonderful and excellent way, as for example, the Gloria in Excelsis, the Alleluia, the Lord's Prayer, the Preface, the Sanctus, the Benedictus, and the Agnus Dei. (AE 38:123)

FROM THE BIBLE

For everything created by God is good, and nothing is to be rejected if it is received with thanksgiving, for it is made holy by the word of God and prayer. (1 Timothy 4:4–5)

TECHNICAL STUFF

"Words of Our Lord" in Latin is *Verba Domini*. Sometimes we refer to them simply as "the *Verba*."

The Words of Our Lord

Jesus gave the Lord's Supper to His Church on the night when He was betrayed. His "Words of Institution" tell us what the gift is and what its benefits are: His true body and blood for the forgiveness of our sins. But these words are more than ancient history. Since Jesus is still among us and speaks through the presiding minister, we call them the **Words of Our Lord**.

The words in our liturgy are a combination of the four biblical accounts of the Last Supper. The pastor speaks them for three reasons:

1. He anchors the Lord's Supper in history by reminding us of the occasion when Jesus instituted it. No man invented this meal, but we pass on what Jesus gave us (1 Corinthians 11:23).
2. He proclaims what Jesus did on the cross and gives in the Sacrament so that the congregation may hear and believe and so receive the Sacrament worthily (1 Corinthians 11:26–29).
3. When the pastor says, "This is My Body" and "This is My Blood," the words do what they say. Jesus works through His powerful Word (John 6:63). The bread and wine become His body and blood for us to eat and drink. We call this the consecration.

When the pastor sings or speaks these words, he will touch the elements and make the sign of the cross over them. These aren't magical gestures, but they aid our faith by pointing out precisely what is being consecrated for us. If the consecrated bread and wine run out before the end of the Distribution, the pastor will repeat Christ's words over the new elements.

Settings One and Two quote two Bible passages after the consecration that remind us of another meaning of this holy meal (1 Corinthians 11:26;

Revelation 22:20). As He comes to us now in the bread and wine, we have confidence to await His coming on the Last Day to save us. So we pray, "Come, Lord Jesus!"

Pax Domini ~ *The Peace of the Lord*

On the evening of the first Easter, Jesus appeared and stood among the disciples gathered in the Upper Room behind locked doors and said, "Peace be with you" (John 20:19). So, also, He miraculously comes to us in the Lord's Supper. He speaks this greeting through the pastor to announce His presence and to remind us that we will receive peace with God through His living body and blood. The appropriate response is "Amen," "I believe it." The **Peace**, which originally took place before the Offertory, was moved to this location in the Western rite in the fifth century.

Agnus Dei ~ *Lamb of God*

The **Agnus Dei** is a threefold repetition of the words of John the Baptist, who pointed to Jesus and said, "Behold, the Lamb of God, who takes away the sin of the world!" (John 1:29). John saw Jesus as the fulfillment of the lambs sacrificed daily in the temple (Exodus 29:38–42), the lamb in the Passover feast (ch. 12), and the suffering lamb prophesied in Isaiah 53. The sins of the world were laid on Jesus at His Baptism and carried to the cross in our place.

The Agnus Dei was introduced into the liturgy in the eighth century for the choir to sing while the consecrated flatbread was broken into pieces for Distribution. It was repeated as long as necessary. In the twelfth century, the Western Church began to use precut wafers. The Agnus Dei was reduced to three repetitions. The Kyrie ("Have mercy on us"), which was sung after each repetition, was replaced at the end with the words "Grant us Thy peace," because it was a time of much warfare.

NEED TO KNOW

The "Words of Institution" were spoken by Jesus at the Last Supper on Holy Thursday. They are recorded in the three Synoptic Gospels and quoted by Paul (Matthew 26:26–28; Mark 14:22–24; Luke 22:19–20; 1 Corinthians 11:23–25).

BELIEVE, TEACH, CONFESS

In the administration of the Holy Supper the words of institution are to be publicly spoken or sung before the congregation distinctly and clearly. . . . The hearers' faith about the nature and fruit of this Sacrament should be aroused, strengthened, and confirmed by Christ's Word. (FC SD VII 79–81)

NEED TO KNOW

Agnus Dei is Latin for "Lamb of God." It refers to the canticle sung at the beginning of the distribution of the Lord's Supper.

WHAT DOES THIS MEAN?

For as soon as Christ says: "This is my body," his body is present through the Word and the power of the Holy Spirit. If the Word is not there, it is mere bread; but as soon as the words are added they bring with them that of which they speak. (AE 36:341)

NEED TO KNOW

Pax Domini is Latin for "the peace of the Lord." It refers to the greetings that the pastor gives immediately after the consecration, holding forth Christ's body and blood just as Jesus showed His resurrected body to the disciples on Easter Eve.

The Agnus Dei is really the first of the Distribution Hymns. It is sung *to* Jesus ("Thou/You"), adoring Him on the altar. It confesses that Jesus is truly present in the bread and wine and that through these gifts, He shows us mercy and gives us peace. We are also reminded that the Divine Service is "the marriage supper of the lamb" (Revelation 19:9).

Distribution

During or after the Agnus Dei, the **Distribution** begins. The pastor, representing Christ as presider, communes himself, any assistants, and then the congregation. When he admits communicants to the altar, the pastor exercises the Office of the Keys.

Jesus broke bread and gave it to His disciples, saying "Take, eat; this is My body." He took the cup and said, "Drink of it, all of you; this cup is the new testament in My blood." When He says, "Do this," He urges us to be faithful to what He said and did.

As he gives out the gifts, the pastor proclaims what we're receiving: "The true body of Christ, given for you." The word *true* emphasizes the real presence in the elements and rejects any

WHAT DOES THIS MEAN?

"The peace of the Lord," etc., which is, so to speak, a public absolution of the sins of the communicants, the true voice of the gospel announcing remission of sins, and therefore the one and most worthy preparation for the Lord's Table, if faith holds to these words as coming from the mouth of Christ himself. (AE 53:28–29) spiritualizing or purely symbolic view of the meal. The communicant says "Amen" to express faith in what is received.

Some Early Church Fathers describe receiving Christ's body in the hand, reverently held like a throne for the King. In the Middle Ages, priests began to place the bread directly into the mouth because some people were taking the host home for superstitious use. Lutherans after the Reformation kept this practice because it so clearly showed that we receive the Sacrament as pure gift. Either way of receiving the consecrated bread can be practiced reverently.

The use of a single cup (chalice) for distributing the precious blood of Jesus has been the Church's universal practice from Christ's institution until the twentieth century. Christ teaches us to hold fast to what He has commanded us to do (Matthew 28:20). Individual cups were introduced in some churches out of a concern for health and hygiene—though there is little evidence that they are safer than the chalice. The Lord promises blessings and life, not harm, to His children who receive His gifts in faith (Matthew 7:7–11; John 6:54). Where individual cups are used, it is particularly important to treat the leftovers reverently.

During the Distribution, Lutherans like to sing hymns that adore Christ and proclaim what is going on in the Sacrament. Those who cannot commune may join in the hymns and pray.

The pastor dismisses the communicants with words that emphasize the blessings of the Sacrament for body and soul. With the words "Depart in peace," he points toward the Nunc Dimittis.

WHAT DOES THIS MEAN?

Particularly the Agnus Dei, above all songs, serves well for the sacrament, for it clearly sings about and praises Christ for having borne our sins and in beautiful, brief words powerfully and sweetly teaches the remembrance of Christ. (AE 38:123)

NEED TO KNOW

The plate that holds the consecrated bread for distribution is called the "paten." It is normally made of silver or gold, appropriate to the precious body of Christ.

NEED TO KNOW

Chalice comes from the Latin word *calix*, meaning "cup." The chalice is usually made of precious materials such as gold and silver, materials that are appropriate for holding the blood of Jesus.

WHAT DOES THIS MEAN?

We must never think of the Sacrament as something harmful from which we had better flee, but as a pure, wholesome, comforting remedy that grants salvation and comfort. It will cure you and give you life both in soul and body. (LC V 68)

NEED TO KNOW

Benedicamus is Latin for "Let us bless [the Lord]," common language in the Psalms for praising God. These words, with the response "Thanks be to God" (Romans 7:25), mark the close of the Divine Service and the daily offices.

Nunc Dimittis ~ *Song of Simeon*

Simeon was an aged and faithful Israelite who waited daily in the temple for the Messiah, because God had promised he wouldn't die until He came. When Mary and Joseph brought the baby Jesus to the temple for His presentation, Simeon took up the baby in his arms and sang what we now call the **Nunc Dimittis** (Luke 2:25–32). He confessed that he was now prepared to die, since he had seen the salvation of Israel.

Since sleep is a biblical image for death, the Nunc Dimittis was traditionally sung in Compline, the night office. Some early Lutherans saw that Simeon's song fit perfectly at the close of Communion (where it is sung in some Eastern rites). For, like Simeon, we have received the very flesh of Jesus and received God's salvation. We leave the altar prepared by God's gifts for eternity with Him.

Settings One and Two provide an alternative Post-Communion Canticle. "Thank the Lord" was written in the 1960s for inclusion in a new hymnal. The text is a loose paraphrase of Psalm 105:1–5.

Post-Communion Collect

Since we have received such a precious gift, we return thanks to God. The **Post-Communion Collect** is a brief concluding table prayer. Setting Three follows Luther's table prayers in the Small Catechism by singing, "O give thanks unto the Lord, for He is good" (Psalm 107:1). The Collect beginning "We give thanks to You" was written by Luther himself. It reminds us that the Lord's Supper strengthens our faith in God and our love for our fellow Christians.

Salutation, Benedicamus, Benediction

With the two great peaks of Word and Sacrament behind us, the liturgical journey concludes swiftly. In Setting Three, the pastor and people repeat once more their intimate greeting in the **Salutation** ("The Lord be with you"). The **Benedicamus** ("Let us bless the Lord") offers a final word of praise and thanks drawn from the Psalms. Historically, this marked the end of Mass if a prayer service followed immediately afterward.

Finally, the pastor speaks the **Benediction**. The ancient service simply ended after Communion with "Depart in peace." In the Middle Ages, the priest added *Ite missa est* ("Go, you are dismissed")—which may be where the word *mass* comes from. Sometimes he also used a trinitarian blessing. It was Luther who suggested using the benediction God gave Aaron the high priest to bestow (Numbers 6:24–26). This is the only benediction actually commanded by God.

The Aaronic benediction connects blessing to the "face" (countenance) of God. Imagine entering a king's throne room and awaiting his attention. When he lifts his face to look at you, you know that he's ready to help. In the Divine Service, we have met the very face of God in Christ Jesus (John 14:9; Colossians 1:15).

The blessing, as the Word of God spoken by Christ's authorized representative, does what it says. It's not a wish or a prayer but an effective blessing. God sends us into the world in His peace and under the protection of His holy triune name. And so the service ends as it began.

WHAT DOES THIS MEAN?

The customary benediction may be given; or else the one from Numbers 6[:24–27], which the Lord himself appointed. . . . I believe Christ used something like this when, ascending into heaven, he blessed his disciples [Luke 24:50–51]. (AE 53:30)

WHAT DOES THIS MEAN?

In Holy Scripture, however, there are real blessings. They are more than mere wishes. They state facts and are effective. They actually bestow and bring what the words say . . . for they are not our works; they are God's works through our ministry. (AE 5:140–41)

Study Questions

1. What aspects of the Preparation Rite remind us of our Baptism? Why is this a good way to enter into God's presence?

2. Why do we use the Psalms in Christian worship? What is their relationship to Jesus?

3. The Kyrie appears near the very beginning of the Divine Service. What does this say about our relationship to God?

4. What is the high point of the Service of the Word? What ceremonial words and actions highlight it?

5. What is a "creed"? What is the origin of the Apostles' and Nicene Creeds?

Visit lutheranism101.com to download the free Leader's Guide.

6. What is unique and useful about the Hymn of the Day?

7. How might both the Prayer of the Church and the offering be seen as responses to the proclamation of God's Word?

8. In what way do the Preface and Proper Preface follow Jesus' own example and command?

9. The Sanctus combines the texts of Isaiah 6:1–3 with Psalm 118:25–26 as sung by the crowds on Palm Sunday. What does the Sanctus teach us about the Lord's Supper?

10. What Old Testament ideas does the Agnus Dei apply to Jesus? What does the Book of Revelation say is going on in heavenly worship?

11. It is said of the Nunc Dimittis that it teaches us to go to the Sacrament as to our death, and to our death as to the Sacrament. How does the Nunc Dimittis do this?

12. What is the difference between a prayer and a blessing? What does the Benediction do?

Discussion Questions

1. Read Revelation 1:1–3; 1 Thessalonians 5:27; 1 Timothy 4:13; and Romans 10:17. Discuss how the reading of Scripture in the Divine Service (not just private reading) is important to the Christian faith.

2. Review Luther's explanation of the Lord's Supper in the Small Catechism, *LSB*, pages 326–27. What does the proclamation of the Words of Our Lord do? Why can they never be omitted from the liturgy?

3. Discuss how the way we observe the Lord's Supper can help confess what is really going on. What practices (posture, gestures, actions) proclaim the real presence of Christ's body and blood?

4. Which parts of the Divine Service teach us that we are joined to the worship of the heavenly hosts? Discuss how this insight can be meaningful and comforting to us living in this troubled world. Why is it important to remember that no single congregation worships alone?

PART THREE

What you'll learn about:

- The rich cycle of festivities in the Church Year
- The space, sights, and sounds of worship
- The involvement of all our senses in the liturgy

God Calls Us in Body, Mind, and Soul

God's Word is absolutely central to Christian worship. But God's Word isn't just for our ears or mind. Through the Sacraments, God's Word touches our bodies, washing us in Baptism and feeding us in the Lord's Supper. It prepares us for the resurrection of the flesh, just as Jesus rose bodily from the grave. The historic liturgy uses physical space, movement, and music to involve our redeemed bodies in God's worship.

CHAPTER 7

The Church Year

In This Chapter

- The origins of the Church Year in the Old and New Testaments
- How Easter is central to the Christian calendar
- The way the Church Year proclaims the life and work of Christ
- How colors and customs can enhance the message of the season

Remembering the Saving Deeds of God

Every family has its story, every community its history. Those stories explain where they've come from and define who they are. Retelling those stories helps to maintain the family's identity and keep it together. This is also why countries observe annual holidays like their independence day or a national day of Thanksgiving.

God created His people Israel through Abraham as their father. He founded them as a nation by redeeming them from Egyptian slavery, giving them His covenant at Sinai, and planting them in the land of Israel. Through His Law, He gave them a regular cycle of observances to remind them of what He had done for them and who they were.

MAKING CONNECTIONS

Family gatherings and national holidays help you to remember who you are. But "Christian" is also who you are. Observing the Church Year—Advent, Christmas, Epiphany, Lent, Easter—in your home can help strengthen this most important identity.

The annual festivals of Passover, Pentecost, and Booths gave them the opportunity to remember God's saving deeds and His ongoing care for them in the Promised Land. Together with the Day of Atonement and the weekly Sabbath, they formed the Church Year of Old Testament Israel.

The Church Year of the New Testament people of God remembers and celebrates the long-awaited fulfillment of these festivals in Jesus Christ (Matthew 5:17; Colossians 2:16). It keeps the Gospel at the center of Christian worship

BELIEVE, TEACH, CONFESS

For ceremonies are needed for this reason alone, that the uneducated be taught ‹what they need to know about Christ›. (AC XXIV 3)

FROM THE BIBLE

I [John] was in the Spirit on the Lord's day. (Revelation 1:10)

BELIEVE, TEACH, CONFESS

We also willingly keep the order of the Mass in the churches, the Lord's Day, and other more famous festival days. With a very grateful mind we include the beneficial and ancient ordinances, especially since they contain a discipline. This discipline is beneficial for educating and training the people. (Ap VII 33)

by keeping the focus on what Christ did for us. Following the Church Year ensures that we hear the whole story of salvation.

Easter Every Sunday

In chapter 4, we learned that early Christians met on Sunday because it was the day when Jesus rose from the dead and appeared in the flesh to the apostles (John 20:19, 26). Before there was an annual Church-Year cycle, the rhythm of Christian worship was weekly. Sunday was and always is a celebration of Easter. Already in the New Testament, Christians were holding their Divine Service every Sunday, at the very least (Acts 20:7; 1 Corinthians 16:2; Revelation 1:10).

The early Christian writer Justin Martyr explains why:

> But Sunday is the day on which we all hold our common assembly, because it is the first day on which God, having wrought a change in the darkness and matter, made the world; and Jesus Christ our Saviour on the same day rose from the dead. (Justin Martyr, *First Apology*, 67)

While we certainly *can* hold the Divine Service on other days, especially in modern times when people are often forced to work on Sundays, we shouldn't let go of the central importance of Sunday.

Times and Seasons

The annual Christian year is divided into three "Times," centered on the great festivals of Christmas, Easter, and Pentecost (see *LSB*, p. x). Each "Time" includes smaller units called "seasons."

- **The Time of Christmas:** Advent, Christmas, and Epiphany seasons
- **The Time of Easter:** Lent, Holy Week, and Easter seasons
- **The Time of the Church:** season after Pentecost

This threefold pattern encourages us to think of the Holy Trinity at work. Although the three persons never do anything alone, we might think of Christmas Time as highlighting the Father, who sent His Son into the world. The Time of Easter focuses on the saving work of Christ at the cross and empty tomb. And the season after Pentecost, the Time of the Church, proclaims the ongoing activity of the Holy Spirit.

Festivals of Christ

Ultimately, though, the Church Year with its major festivals is all about Christ. **Christmas** proclaims His birth in the flesh. **Easter** celebrates His resurrection from the dead. And **Pentecost** is the fulfillment of His promise to send the Holy Spirit. Since these three major festivals fall in the first half of the Church Year, we call it the "festival half." While modern culture has inflated Christmas into an overwhelming holiday, the historic Christian Church has always viewed Easter as the highest festival. If the Church Year (like the Divine Service) is seen as a mountain range, the festival half has three outstanding peaks—with Easter the highest and most magnificent.

Seasons

For anyone living any distance from the equator, the tilted earth's annual trip around the sun gives four distinct seasons. Each has a certain look. Spring is bright green and colorful. Summer's greens are rich and lush. Autumn brings red and then brown. Winter is bare and often white. And each season has its mood, whether lazy summer or brutal winter.

The seasons of the Church Year also have their colors and moods. In the Middle Ages, churches would bring out the finest materials for vestments and paraments on high festivals. Dark colors (black, brown, blue, violet) were used for penitential seasons. By the sixteenth century—the time of the Reformation—the Western Church had settled on a sequence of four basic colors: white for festivals of Christ and saints' days, red for Pentecost and martyrs, violet for penitential Advent and Lent, and green as a neutral color for other times. Other colors have been added here and there in the twentieth century such as blue for Advent, gold for Easter Sunday, and scarlet for Holy Week.

The cycle of colors can create a dramatic change of mood that helps the

The Church-Year Cycle

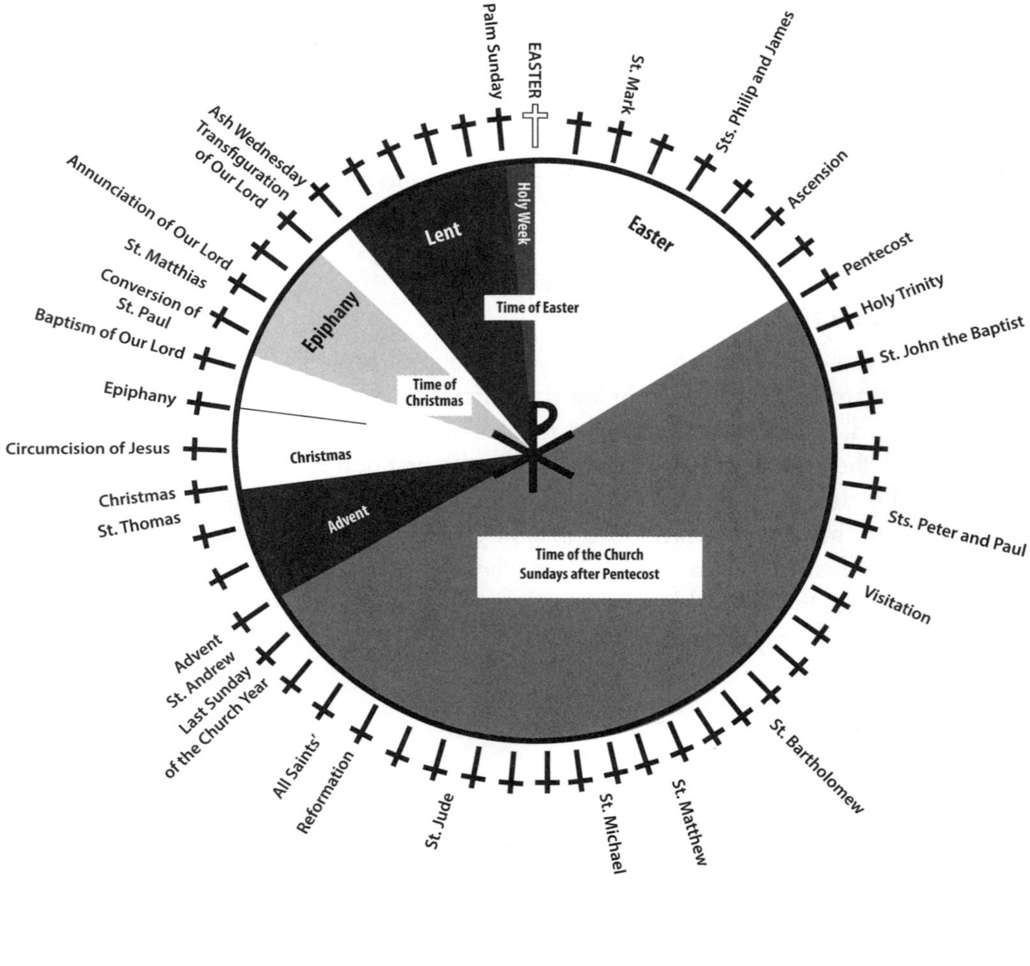

Palm Sunday
EASTER
St. Mark
Sts. Philip and James
Ascension
Pentecost
Holy Trinity
St. John the Baptist
Sts. Peter and Paul
Visitation
St. Bartholomew
St. Matthew
St. Michael
St. Jude
Reformation
All Saints'
Last Sunday of the Church Year
St. Andrew
Advent
St. Thomas
Christmas
Circumcision of Jesus
Epiphany
Baptism of Our Lord
Conversion of St. Paul
St. Matthias
Annunciation of Our Lord
Transfiguration of Our Lord
Ash Wednesday
Holy Week
Lent
Easter
Time of Easter
Epiphany
Time of Christmas
Christmas
Advent
Time of the Church
Sundays after Pentecost

TIMELINE

Advent
CHRISTMAS
Epiphany
Lent
Holy Week
EASTER
Pentecost
Sundays after Pentecost

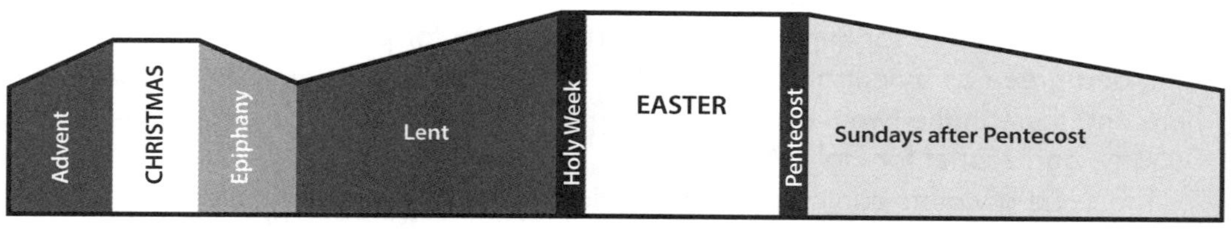

congregation grasp the message of the readings and hymns in the liturgy. The customs of the seasons make the transitions even more moving, as no flowers or Alleluia in Lent makes Easter so much more joyful when they return. Sights, sounds, and movement combine to engage the worshipers' bodies as well as their minds in the annual march from Christ's incarnation to His second coming.

NEED TO KNOW

Advent comes from the Latin for "coming." The season focuses on Christ's first coming at Christmas, His second coming on the Last Day, and His coming in between by Word and Sacrament.

Advent

Advent is a time of preparation for Christmas. But as we prepare to celebrate the first coming of Christ in the flesh, we also think of His second coming in rescue and judgment. This gives Advent the twin themes of hope and repentance (1 Peter 1:13–16; 2 Peter 3:11–14). The best way to be prepared is through listening to God's Word and receiving Christ when He comes to us in the flesh already now in His Supper.

Advent began in Gaul in the fifth century as a forty-day penitential season like Lent. Rome observed a more joyful four-week preparation for Christmas. Eventually the two approaches merged to give us our four-week Advent with both penitential and hopeful aspects. In the twentieth century, blue became a popular alternative to violet to differentiate Advent from Lent.

In our contemporary culture, it's difficult to resist the pressure to bring Christmas into Advent. But there are great spiritual blessings in letting Advent have its way. Its four Sundays proclaim the prophecies of Christ's birth, the angelic messages to Joseph and Mary, and the firm promises of His return on the Last Day. The Advent wreath with its four candles helps us count the time. We omit the Gloria in Excelsis so that this song of the angels is heard afresh in celebration of its first singing on Christmas Eve.

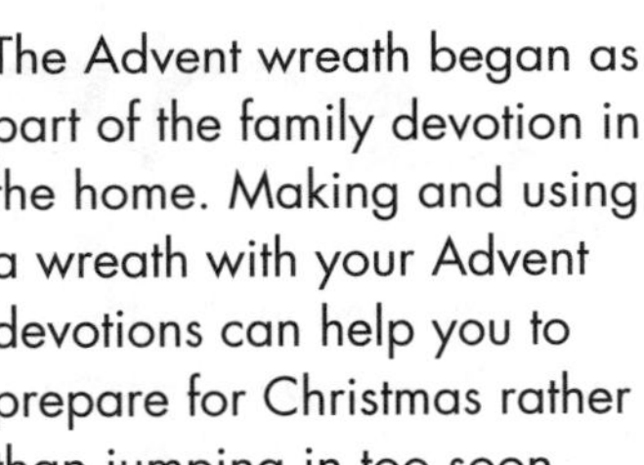

MAKING CONNECTIONS

The Advent wreath began as part of the family devotion in the home. Making and using a wreath with your Advent devotions can help you to prepare for Christmas rather than jumping in too soon.

FROM THE BIBLE

For the grace of God has appeared, bringing salvation for all people, training us to renounce ungodliness and worldly passions, and to live self-controlled, upright, and godly lives in the present age, waiting for our blessed hope, the appearing of the glory of our great God and Savior Jesus Christ. (Titus 2:11–13)

FROM THE BIBLE

And suddenly there was with the angel a multitude of the heavenly host praising God and saying, "Glory to God in the highest, and on earth peace among those with whom He is pleased!" (Luke 2:13–14)

TECHNICAL STUFF

Incarnation means "in the flesh." It describes the way the Son of God took on human flesh in the womb of Mary and was born as the God-man, Jesus.

NEED TO KNOW

Christmas is a contraction of "Christ's mass" and refers to the Divine Service in celebration of His birth. The abbreviation *Xmas* uses *chi* (X), the first letter of the word *Christ* in Greek.

Christmas

Every year, the secular media claim that Christmas is based on pagan sun-god worship, and that no one really knows when Jesus was born anyway. This simply isn't true. Christians were celebrating Christ's birth already in the third century, before the popularity of the sun cult and before Christianity became a state religion. Most likely they preserved the true tradition of when He was born.

Early Christians celebrated on one day (January 6) all the events of Christ's incarnation—His birth, circumcision, visit by the Magi, and Baptism. In the fourth century, the Church separated these events by moving Christmas Day forward to December 25. Our twelve-day Christmas celebration includes all these festivals, as well as the feast days of St. Stephen, St. John, and Holy Innocents (the slaughter of the Bethlehem babies), and concludes on the eve of Epiphany. While we treasure our cultural traditions of gift-giving and family gatherings, the way to receive spiritual benefit from Christmas is to be part of the rich liturgical festivities that last for twelve full days.

The seasonal color white represents the pure glory of Christ and the angels. Candles on Christmas Eve remind us that Christ came in darkest night to be the light of the world (John 1:9). The Christmas tree is an ancient symbol of Christ, who is the tree of life (Ezekiel 17:22; Revelation 22:2). In the Middle Ages, it was decorated with baubles to look like fruit and symbols made of dried bread to remind us that Christ feeds us with His body in the Lord's Supper.

Epiphany

Epiphany (January 6) celebrates the coming of the Magi (Wise Men) to worship the baby Jesus (Matthew 2:1–12). Because God led them by a star, the star is the chief symbol of this season.

At Christmas, Jesus was revealed to shepherds as representatives of Israel. The Wise Men represent the revelation of Jesus to the Gentile world as God in the flesh.

On the First Sunday after the Epiphany, the season continues with the Baptism of Our Lord, when Christ was anointed for His messianic office and declared to be God's Son (Matthew 3:13–17). Jesus' miracle of turning water into wine at the Cana wedding (John 2:1–12) is the traditional reading for the next Sunday. The Epiphany season focuses on Jesus' miracles, which reveal His divinity and are "signs" pointing to the truth of His Word. The final Sunday after Epiphany is the Transfiguration of Our Lord, when Jesus gives a brief glimpse of His divine glory before heading to the cross.

The color white is used for the festival days at the beginning and end of the season, portraying Jesus' divine glory. On the Sundays in between, the color green is used. In the early part of Epiphany, it is traditional to keep singing Christmas carols. This extension of Christmas ends on February 2, when we celebrate the Presentation of Our Lord in the temple (Luke 2:22–39). This was when Simeon sang his Nunc Dimittis.

Lent

We tend to think of Lent as a time of preparation for Easter—which it is. But Lent has its own unique character. In the first four centuries of Christianity, it was normal to hold Baptisms on the night before Easter (the Vigil). Lent was the time for final "catechesis" or instruction preparing candidates for Baptism. By the early Middle Ages, it was rare for anyone to enter Christianity as an adult convert. Lent then became a time of repentance for people who had been excommunicated and wished to repent and be forgiven in time to commune at Easter. At the beginning of the season, they put on sackcloth and ashes, which is the origin of Ash Wednesday.

MAKING CONNECTIONS

The twelve days of Christmas can be a rich part of your family devotions and customs. Think about giving a little gift on each day or at least saving a gift for Epiphany Eve to remind your family of the abundance of God's gifts in Christ. And keep on singing carols!

NEED TO KNOW

Epiphany comes from a Greek word that means "appearance." In the New Testament, it refers to Christ's first and second comings.

FROM THE BIBLE

Henceforth there is laid up for me the crown of righteousness, which the Lord, the righteous judge, will award to me on that day, and not only to me but also to all who have loved His appearing [*epiphany*]. (2 Timothy 4:8)

This time of repentance and spiritual renewal was eventually extended to all Christians. It is forty days long to parallel Jesus' forty days of fasting and prayer in the wilderness after His Baptism (Matthew 4:2). It also reminds us soberly of the forty-day flood and Israel's forty years in the wilderness. Although Sundays are always celebrations of Easter, and so not properly part of Lent, we tend to observe Lenten customs on Sundays because our people may not get much of Lent otherwise. We omit the Gloria in Excelsis and Alleluia and have no flowers at the altar so that Easter will seem all the more joyful when they return. Violet, the color used during Lent, is penitential, but it also reminds us of the mocking royal robe placed on Jesus by the soldiers (Mark 15:17).

Holy Week focuses more keenly on Christ's sufferings. Following customs observed in ancient Jerusalem, we walk in Jesus' footsteps by remembering His triumphant entry on Palm Sunday, His institution of the Lord's Supper on Holy Thursday, His crucifixion on Good Friday, and His rest in the tomb on Holy Saturday. On Palm Sunday—also known as the Sunday of the Passion—we read the full story of Holy Week from one of the Synoptic Gospels, and we read John's account on Good Friday. We immerse ourselves in the suffering and death of Christ that was made our own in Baptism.

MAKING CONNECTIONS

You can make use of Lent as a time of spiritual renewal by committing yourself to more intense Bible reading and prayer. Fasting can help you focus on eternal nourishment. Likewise, charitable giving can help break your attachment to this world and benefit your neighbor. See Matthew 6.

NEED TO KNOW

Lent is an old English word meaning "spring," the time when the days "lengthen." It refers to the forty-day period before Easter, excluding Sundays.

TECHNICAL STUFF

The Latin name for Lent is *Quadragesima*, meaning "forty days" (Ash Wednesday to Holy Saturday, excluding Sundays). The medieval calendar added three Sundays of "Pre-Lent," preserved in the *LSB One-Year Lectionary*: *Septuagesima*, *Sexagesima*, and *Quinquagesima*, meaning seventy, sixty, and fifty days before Easter. Since our weeks are not ten days long, none of these are really good math!

Easter

Jesus was crucified on the day after Passover; the Scriptures see Easter as the fulfillment of that festival. At Easter, Jesus delivered us from our slavery to sin. Jesus is our Passover Lamb, who during the Passover meal first gave His body and blood for us to eat and drink. Early Christians called the whole festival, from Christ's death to His resurrection, *Pascha*, which is Greek for Passover. For many centuries, they celebrated all the events of Holy Week in a vigil from Saturday dusk until Sunday dawn, when they celebrated the resurrection with the Lord's Supper. Since the fourth century, Christians have separated these events into the eight days of Holy Week, but *LSB* still provides an "Easter Vigil" service for Saturday night. The Vigil focuses on Baptism, through which we join Jesus in His death and resurrection.

As Easter is the greatest festival of the Church Year, we celebrate it for a full fifty days, ending on Pentecost. The season embraces the forty days of Jesus' earthly walk with the disciples in His resurrected flesh, when He taught them the meaning of His death and resurrection (Acts 1:3). On the fortieth day—always a Thursday—we celebrate His ascension to reign at the right hand of God. Jesus isn't gone but fills the universe and comes to us through His Word and Sacrament (Ephesians 1:20–23).

The color of the Easter season is white, representing the glory of Jesus' resurrected body. When the altar is stripped for Good Friday, its

FROM THE BIBLE

Christ, our Passover lamb [*Pascha*], has been sacrificed. Let us therefore celebrate the festival, not with the old leaven, the leaven of malice and evil, but with the unleavened bread of sincerity and truth. (1 Corinthians 5:7–8)

MAKING CONNECTIONS

How can your family's Easter customs focus on its *Christian* meaning? The Easter egg is an ancient symbol of Christ's breaking forth from the tomb, but the Easter bunny is a distraction from the true faith. Hot-*cross* buns give a joyful way to celebrate Christ's victory over death. Make Easter with its joyful hymns part of your devotions for the full fifty days.

TECHNICAL STUFF

Holy Week culminates with the "Triduum," which means "three days." This refers to the services from Holy Thursday (the Eve of Good Friday) until Easter Sunday, which can be seen as one long observance of Christ's Passion.

decoration with the finest paraments and flowers on Easter Sunday makes a stunning contrast. We restore the Alleluia to the liturgy and sing again the Gloria in Excelsis or "This Is the Feast." The paschal candle with its unique symbols is lit at the Easter Vigil and remains lit for all services until the end of the Easter season (Pentecost). It symbolizes the resurrected life of Jesus, and so is lit also for Baptisms and funerals as a witness to the resurrection of our flesh. During the Easter season, it is traditional to stand for prayer (rather than kneeling) as a confession of the resurrection, and there is no fasting.

Pentecost

Luke records that during the celebration of the Old Testament festival of Pentecost (Leviticus 23:15–21), the Holy Spirit was poured out on Jesus' disciples in a visible and extraordinary way. They spoke in many languages so that worshipers from all over the world heard and believed the Gospel and were baptized (Acts 2). While it was not the birth of the Christian Church, it was a miraculous explosion, as they carried the message far and wide.

We celebrate Pentecost as the completion of the Easter season and the fulfillment of Jesus' promise that He will send the Holy Spirit to His Church (John 14:15–31; 16:5–7). Pentecost is a celebration of the Spirit's work, particularly in creating faith in the heart through Holy Baptism and preaching (Acts 2:38). But the Spirit's work is to point not to Himself, but to Jesus (John 15:26). So Pentecost is still a festival of Christ.

The Christian Church has celebrated Pentecost since at least the third century, perhaps already in apostolic times (Acts 20:16). The color of Pentecost is red, recalling the tongues of fire on the disciples (2:3).

TECHNICAL STUFF

In order to keep Easter in the spring and close to its original date, early Christians established a rule: Easter is celebrated on the first Sunday after the first full moon that occurs on or after March 21. Thus Easter can fall on any Sunday between March 22 and April 25. Eastern Christians follow the same rule, but they use the ancient Julian calendar (which is thirteen days late); their Easter can be weeks later than in the West.

NEED TO KNOW

Easter is an old English word derived from the name of the pagan goddess Eostre, who had a spring festival in pre-Christian Britain. In most other languages, the name for Easter comes from the biblical word *Pascha* (Passover).

After Pentecost

When Pentecost is over, the festival half of the Church Year is complete. The next Sunday has been dedicated to the doctrine of the Holy Trinity since the tenth century. The color is white and the lengthy and detailed Athanasian Creed is usually confessed. On the Sunday after Trinity, the color becomes green—the neutral color, representing life and growth—until the end of the Church Year.

In this "Time of the Church," the readings from the Gospel take us through the work and teachings of Jesus. The Epistle often reads continuously through a letter. In this way, we receive "the whole counsel of God" (Acts 20:27).

From the festival of St. Michael and All Angels (September 29) onward, the Time of the Church becomes decidedly "eschatological." Coming during harvest time, this festival recalls Jesus' teaching that on the Last Day, He will send the holy angels to gather the elect into His kingdom (Matthew 24:31). From then until the end of the Church Year, we focus on repentance and hope as we learn about the end times and await Christ's return. The Last Sunday of the Church Year is a liturgical enactment of the Last Day itself, when Christ comes to judge the world and redeem His people.

In this way, the Church Year ends where it began, as the Last Sunday leads us into Advent and the hope that the first coming of Christ gave us.

Feasts and Festivals

Superimposed over the annual cycle of the Church Year are individual "feasts" of Christ and other "festivals" (see *LSB*, p. xi). While the Sundays of the Church Year move around depending on when Easter falls, feasts and festivals are fixed to specific calendar dates. The word *feast* reminds us that it is appropriate to celebrate these high occasions with the Lord's Supper.

TECHNICAL STUFF

In the late Middle Ages, the Sundays after Pentecost came to be called Sundays "after Trinity," as in the *LSB One-Year Lectionary*. In the twentieth century, the Three-Year Lectionary restored the older designation, since Pentecost is a greater festival. Sundays numbered "after Trinity" will always be lower by one.

TECHNICAL STUFF

Eschatology comes from Greek words that mean "the study of end times." It refers to the biblical teachings about what happens as the end of the world draws close and Christ returns.

BELIEVE, TEACH, CONFESS

Masses are celebrated among us every Lord's Day and on the other festivals. The Sacrament is offered to those who wish to use it, after they have been examined and absolved. (Ap XXIV 1)

The Feasts of Christ

The Feasts of Christ include major events in His life that may not fit into the normal flow of the Church Year. At times, however, they take on added meaning because of the season where they fall. For example, we observe the Annunciation of Our Lord—when the angel announced to Mary that she was pregnant with Jesus—on March 25, nine months before Christmas. The Ancient Church believed this was the original date of Good Friday. This reminds us *why* Jesus took on human flesh: to die for us.

The Feasts of Christ include the following:

- The Circumcision and Name of Jesus (January 1)
- The Purification of Mary and the Presentation of Our Lord (February 2)
- The Annunciation of Our Lord (March 25)
- The Visitation of Mary with Elizabeth (May 31 or July 2)

Festivals of the Saints

Saint is a biblical word meaning "holy person" and refers to all Christians who have been made holy through Baptism (1 Corinthians 1:2). But we also use the word to refer to particularly significant figures in the Church's history. In the Early Church, which suffered much persecution, Christians treasured the bodies of local martyrs. They sometimes buried them under the altar and remembered their courageous confession each year on the anniversary of their death. This is the origin of saints' days.

In the Middle Ages, the number of saints' days multiplied out of control. The Lutheran reformers thought these days were overwhelming the Christ-centered Church Year, and they objected to calling on saints for help. So they reduced the number of saints' days to just the biblical saints, such as the apostles and Mary. *LSB* distinguishes between these primary saints' days and "commemorations" of other saints from Church history.

The Apology of the Augsburg Confession (Ap XXI 4–6) encourages us to remember the saints for three reasons:

1. to give thanks to God for these examples of His mercy;
2. to strengthen our faith when we see how God's grace abounded in their lives; and
3. to provide strong examples for Christians to imitate in faith and other virtues.

The color for saints who died a natural death is white. For martyrs, the color is red, not only because they spilled their blood, but also to remind us that the Holy Spirit of Pentecost gave them the courage to confess.

Lectionary

The Church Year is guided by the lectionary, which gives a set of readings appointed for each Sunday and festival (*LSB*, xiv–xxiii). The Jews in New Testament times had an ordered way of reading through the Pentateuch and the prophets in the synagogue (Acts 13:15). Early Christians kept reading the Old Testament in this way, but they added readings from the Gospels and Epistles.

By the seventh century, the Old Testament Reading disappeared, probably because of a misunderstanding of its Christian meaning. The "historic lectionary" of the Middle Ages was a one-year cycle of readings from an Epistle and Gospel. Early Lutherans kept the lectionary but adjusted the readings slightly to highlight justification by faith. The Old Testament Reading wasn't widely restored until the twentieth century.

LSB preserves a form of the one-year historic lectionary. Its advantages included getting to know a core of the most important biblical texts and having musical and preaching resources based on those texts from Church history.

The three-year lectionary was developed in the 1960s to give the Church a broader exposure to the Bible. The three years (A, B, C) focus on Matthew, Mark, and Luke respectively, with John spread throughout. The three-year lectionary in *LSB* is based on the *Revised Common Lectionary* (1992), now used by the majority of Western Christians. The Old Testament Reading usually coordinates with the Holy Gospel by providing a prophecy or type of Jesus. The Epistle may also fit the Gospel but sometimes just reads through a letter continuously.

The lectionary is valuable in many ways:

- It protects the church from the pastor's whims and failings.
- It stops us from choosing only the bits of God's Word we want to hear.
- It helps us hear the full counsel of God and the whole life of Christ.
- It highlights the central message of Scripture.
- It helps us find Christ in the Old Testament by connecting it to the Gospels.
- It unites Christians in the whole Church.
- It saves an enormous amount of time creating a scheme of our own!

FROM THE BIBLE

As was His custom, He went to the synagogue on the Sabbath day, and He stood up to read. And the scroll of the prophet Isaiah was given to Him. (Luke 4:16–17)

BELIEVE, TEACH, CONFESS

Nevertheless, we keep many traditions that are leading to good order [1 Corinthians 14:40] in the Church, such as the order of Scripture lessons in the Mass and the chief holy days. (AC XXVI 40)

The lectionary is also the name of a book that contains the readings organized by Sunday and festival. The lectionary helps the reader find the readings quickly and is printed in a large typeface. Historically, lectionaries were richly decorated with precious metals and jewels appropriate to a book containing the very Word of God. The beauty of the book from which we read can help faith grasp what it's receiving.

Study Questions

1. What does every Sunday commemorate?

2. What is the highest festival of the Church Year? Why?

3. What are the twin themes of Advent? What three comings of Christ does Advent proclaim?

4. What can the Christmas tree teach us?

5. What two main things are "revealed" in the Epiphany season?

6. How was Lent originally connected with Baptism? Why is it helpful for us to observe Lent today?

Visit lutheranism101.com to download the free Leader's Guide.

7. What does the word *Pascha* mean? What does it tell us about Easter?

8. In what way is Pentecost not only a festival of the Holy Spirit but also of Christ?

9. What does the use of the color green during the Time of the Church teach us?

10. Why is it helpful to use a lectionary rather than decide for ourselves what Scripture to read in church?

Discussion Questions

1. In chapter 3, we said that Christian worship is always both trinitarian and Christological. Discuss how the Church Year follows that same pattern. See *LSB*, page x, to understand better the organization of the Church Year.

2. Discuss what the change of seasons is like in the part of the world where you live. What do the seasons mean to nature? How do they affect you? Now consider how the Church Year's annual cycle with its change of seasons can be meaningful.

3. How has the celebration of Christmas changed in your own lifetime? What do we lose when it overruns Advent and then promptly fizzles out on December 26?

4. Discuss the variety of observances that make up Holy Week and the Triduum. How might you give more prominence to Easter in your church by expanding or enriching your use of these services?

5. Talk about the observance of saints' days in your church. Is there a "Lutheran" way to remember the saints? How is it different from the Roman Catholic cult of the saints, on the one hand, and Pentecostal-style "testimonies," on the other?

CHAPTER 8

Signs and Ceremonies

In This Chapter

- How space and furnishings in the church serve the liturgy
- Why we put special clothes on the pastor and the church furniture
- The rich ways music can lift our hearts and serve God's Word
- How we express the faith through posture and gesture

Art and Architecture

Holy Space for Holy Things

Although God is present everywhere, the church building is holy space because God is there in a unique way to give out His holy gifts of Word and Sacrament. This means that true worship can take place anywhere these gifts are given, no matter how plain or simple the space (John 4:19–24). But as Christians receive those holy gifts in faith, their thankfulness leads them to think about how the space itself can give praise to God and serve His gifts. When you look at your church or make plans to renovate or build a new one, consider how its design can suit its purpose.

A church building needs to be large enough to accommodate the gathered congregation but intimate enough that everyone can see and hear what's happening. The church isn't a living room meant for people to just sit and be comfortable. The liturgy calls on people to stand, walk, kneel, process, speak, sing, and listen. It's easiest for the pastor's preaching to be heard if he has an elevated place to stand. The prayers can draw in the people if the altar is high and visible. Hard surfaces like stone and wood (rather than stucco and carpeting) make it a joy to sing and listen, so that we feel part of a great host of worshipers. A tall church not only lets sound resonate but also lifts our eyes to heaven.

But, as we observed in the Introduction, the space of worship can be so much more than just practical. It tells us what is going on. We ought to know immediately that we're in the house of God. The church provides locations for each Means of

Grace and holds them always before our eyes. So the font recalls our Baptism even when it isn't being used.

Beauty and Glory

The artful adornment of the church can be part of our doxology. As the Israelites donated gold, jewels, and fine fabrics to adorn the tabernacle (Exodus 25:1–9), so we can worship God by making His place of worship precious and beautiful. It's an offering that expresses our faith and devotion (John 12:1–7). And it creates a space that can proclaim God's glory.

In the Old Testament, God's people were forbidden to make images of Him like pagan idolaters. But since the Son of God took on human flesh and showed us the very face of God (Colossians 1:15), we are free to depict Christ in art. The crucifix displays Christ's body on the cross, proclaiming the Gospel (1 Corinthians 1:23) and reminding us that Christ is truly among us in the flesh. Mosaics, paintings, and stained glass windows can portray biblical stories in a way that enhances the preached Word and glorifies God.

FROM THE BIBLE

He is the image of the invisible God, the firstborn of all creation. (Colossians 1:15)

TECHNICAL STUFF

The baptismal font is normally made with eight sides. Baptism is the fulfillment of circumcision on the eighth day; and Christ rose on Sunday, the eighth day and the start of a new creation. Noah's ark, which was a type of Baptism, saved eight people. (1 Peter 3:20)

Ordered Space

Christian churches were traditionally built with the entrance in the west and the altar in the east (when this can't be done, we refer to the "liturgical east"). The congregation faces east to await the coming of Christ on the Last Day like the rising of the sun (Matthew 24:27).

As you enter a Christian church from the west door, you will encounter the following:

Narthex: The entrance area that forms a transition between the world and the church. It gives space to prepare for worship, to gather for processions, and to greet one another.

Font: The place to hold water for Holy Baptism. It may be located at the back of the church to symbolize entrance into the faith, or up front to portray the path to the Lord's Supper. Historically, it was often located in a separate building called a baptistery.

Nave: The body of the building where the worshipers gather. It comes from the Latin word for "ship," comparing the church to Noah's ark (1 Peter 3:20).

Transcept: Some churches, when viewed from above, are shaped like a cross. The transcept is the crossing, with arms to each side where worshipers or musicians may sit.

Chancel: The area at the front of the church where the pastor presides and the people come for the Lord's Supper. It may be divided into a **sanctuary** (altar area) and **choir** (seating area for the choir).

Pulpit: An elevated speaking platform normally used only for the sermon, but also for the readings if there is no lectern.

Lectern: A podium for reading the Holy Scriptures.

Altar: In the Old Testament, the altar was the place where sacrifices were offered to God. Since Jesus, through His death on the cross, is the once-for-all sacrifice, we center our worship on an altar to remember His sacrifice, to receive the benefits of His sacrifice in the Lord's Supper (Hebrews 13:10), and to offer spiritual sacrifices of prayer and praise through Him (1 Peter 2:5).

Vestments and Paraments

The high priest in the Old Testament wore beautiful and precious vestments suited for the dramatic significance of his work. Twelve jewels on his breastplate showed that he represented all Israel in his liturgical work (Exodus 28). Since Christ fulfilled this work (Hebrews 9:11–12), the Early Christian Church didn't try to reproduce the priestly garments on their ministers. But from earliest days, it appears that Christian ministers didn't simply wear their street clothes when presiding over the holy things. As mature men, they normally wore a long, dignified robe. For a liturgical service, it would be made of white linen. The white robe symbolized the righteousness of Christ that is put on us in Holy Baptism (Luke 15:22–23; Galatians 3:27; Revelation 7:13–14). No one can stand before a holy God unless he has been made holy. By the fifth century, when trousers from northern Europe became popular, the long liturgical robe became more distinctive.

Vestments became more elaborate after Constantine's conversion brought wealth and status to the Church, but their basic meaning remained the same. Vestments cover up the individual man and highlight the office he exercises. Vestments are a visual reminder that the minister represents Christ and stands in the apostolic office, as he wears garments similar to what they wore. Differences in vestments can help worshipers understand who is doing what in the service.

BELIEVE, TEACH, CONFESS

[Paul teaches] that the office of the ministry proceeds from the general call of the apostles. (Tr 10)

BELIEVE, TEACH, CONFESS

And the usual public ceremonies are observed, the series of lessons, of prayers, vestments, and other such things. (Ap XXIV 1)

While early Lutherans may have scoffed at some of the pompous displays put on by medieval clergy, the Lutheran Reformation retained vestments as helpful for the church and a mark of continuity with historic Christianity. Some Lutherans adopted the Reformed practice of wearing just a black gown (based on academic dress), but in the twentieth century, most Lutherans restored the traditional vestments.

Dressing the Man

The basic outfit for a minister presiding at the Lord's Supper is an alb with cincture, a stole, and a chasuble—although the chasuble is not worn in all Lutheran churches. Some ministers follow the tradition of wearing the cassock and surplice for non-Communion services; it can be more graceful looking than an alb alone.

Vestments used in a typical Lutheran church may include the following:

Alb: The long, white linen robe derived from ancient Greco-Roman dress, whose name derives from the Latin *tunica alba*, meaning "white robe." It is the basic liturgical garment for all ministers and assistants.

Cincture: A rope or fabric belt worn around the waist of an alb or cassock.

Cassock: A long, tight-fitting black robe that was adopted as the ordinary street dress of clergy when the fashion turned to shorter robes and trousers in late antiquity. Today, the black **clerical shirt** serves the same function.

Surplice: A looser-fitting version of the alb developed in northern Europe to fit over a fur-lined cassock.

Stole: A long, scarf-like vestment in the color of the Church season, worn around the neck and hanging in front over an alb or surplice. It is a mark of office that identifies the minister as an ordained man.

Chasuble: An ample round vestment developed from the ancient cloak or outer garment (2 Timothy 4:13). The word *chasuble* comes from the Latin *casula*, meaning "little house." Made in the color of the season, it is worn over the alb and stole to mark the presider at the Lord's Supper.

Dressing the Place

Paraments not only adorn the chancel but also help set the mood with their seasonal colors and symbols. They include the following:

Frontal: A decorated fabric in the color of the season that hangs on the front of the altar. The pulpit and lectern may also have frontals or **antependia**.

Fair linen: A long, rectangular white linen embroidered with five crosses (representing the wounds of Christ) that covers the top of the altar and hangs down the sides. It represents the shroud left in the tomb by the resurrected Christ (John 20:6–7).

Chalice veil: A covering for the chalice and paten (Communion vessels) that may be plain white linen or made in the color of the season.

Funeral pall: A parament that completely covers the coffin at a funeral. Normally white with cross-shaped decorative bands, it represents the righteousness of Christ that covers one who has been baptized.

WHAT DOES THIS MEAN?

There is to be neither commanding nor forbidding, neither to the right nor to the left. . . . For in the cloister we observed mass without chasuble, without elevation, in the most plain and simple way. . . . On the other hand, in the parish church we still have the chasuble, alb, altar, and elevate [the host] as long as it pleases us. (AE 40:130)

NEED TO KNOW

Paraments is a general name for cloth coverings on the altar, pulpit, and lectern, normally in the color of the Church season.

Music

Writing just a generation after the apostles, the Church Father Ignatius conjured the image of strings on a harp to describe the unity of the ministers and the people in the liturgical gathering:

> You must join in this chorus, every one of you, so that by being harmonious in love and taking up the song of God in unison, you may with one voice sing to the Father through Jesus Christ, so that He may both hear you, and . . . acknowledge that you are indeed members of his Son. (Ignatius, *To the Ephesians*, 4:2)

Ignatius isn't forbidding four-part harmony in church! He's recognizing the power of music to draw a congregation's worship into unity. Music helps the church speak with one voice, which gives spectacular witness to the truth that our worship is given to the Father through Jesus Christ alone.

Wherever God's people have gathered for worship, there has been music. Music has the power to lift up heart, mind, and soul to God, to stir the emotions toward joy or sorrow. Martin Luther stated numerous times that music is an outstanding and great gift of God. He placed it next to theology and gave it the highest praise. Therefore, it is not surprising that music is the greatest servant of God's Word. And from the very beginning, Lutherans have been known as the singing church!

The Biblical Basis of Music

Whenever God acted mightily to redeem His people, they responded with songs of praise and thanks. Safe on the shores of the Red Sea, Moses celebrated Israel's rescue by singing, declaring that God Himself *is* their song (Exodus 15). When God established the liturgy of the tabernacle and temple, He appointed the Levites as musicians. King David organized the Levites into divisions with musical directors and composers at the head (1 Chronicles 15, 25). Playing instruments and forming choirs, they assembled by the altar to accompany the sacrifices with songs of praise (23:30–31).

The Book of Psalms formed the hymnal of public worship in the temple—the word *psalm* means "song." King David, who wrote many of the psalms, was an accomplished lyre player (1 Samuel 16:23). Fifty-five psalms are dedicated "to the choirmaster," often with instruments specified (e.g., Psalm 4:1). The psalm that crowns the collection celebrates the central role of instrumental music in temple worship (Psalm 150).

WHAT DOES THIS MEAN?

Next to the Word of God, music deserves the highest praise. . . . For whether you wish to comfort the sad, to terrify the happy, to encourage the despairing, to humble the proud, to calm the passionate, or to appease those full of hate . . . what more effective means than music could you find? (AE 53:323)

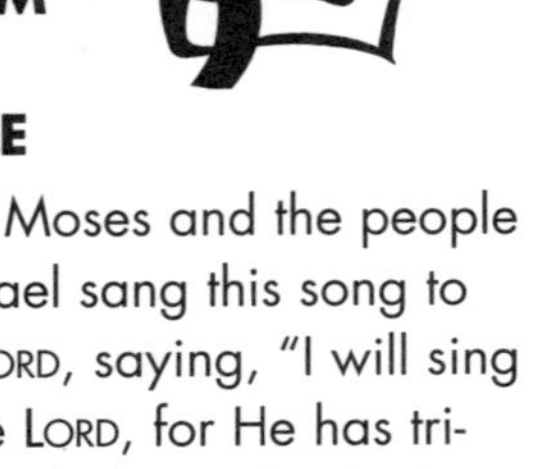

FROM THE BIBLE

Then Moses and the people of Israel sang this song to the LORD, saying, "I will sing to the LORD, for He has triumphed gloriously; the horse and his rider He has thrown into the sea. The LORD is my strength and my song, and He has become my salvation." (Exodus 15:1–2)

The New Testament draws music into the worship of God the Father through Christ. Music lifts the Christian celebration of God's ultimate act of deliverance. We have no melodies preserved from early Christianity—they probably continued the Jewish style of rhythmic chant. But we know they continued to sing the Psalms, and in the New Testament we find some early Christian hymn texts (Ephesians 5:14; 1 Timothy 3:16), as well as heavenly songs (Revelation 5:12). But most important is why and to whom they sang:

> Be filled up in the Spirit, speaking to one another in psalms and hymns and songs of the Spirit, singing and psalming with your heart to the Lord, giving thanks always for all things in the name of our Lord Jesus Christ to [our] God and Father. (Ephesians 5:18b–20, author's translation)

FROM THE BIBLE

And all the Levitical singers . . . arrayed in fine linen, with cymbals, harps, and lyres, stood east of the altar with 120 priests who were trumpeters; and it was the duty of the trumpeters and singers to make themselves heard in unison in praise and thanksgiving to the LORD. (2 Chronicles 5:12–13)

FROM THE BIBLE

Make a joyful noise to the LORD, all the earth! Serve the LORD with gladness! Come into His presence with singing! (Psalm 100:1–2)

The Music of the Congregation

In the Middle Ages, the congregation slowly lost its involvement in singing the liturgy. Only the choir could handle the Latin texts and complicated musical settings. The Lutheran Reformation gradually developed simpler musical settings and vernacular translations that allowed the people again to sing the liturgy. *LSB* provides musical settings of the canticles, psalms, and responses that are meant to be beautiful and durable, yet simple enough for anyone to learn.

From earliest days, Christians responded to the Word of God by writing hymns. The oldest hymn in *LSB* comes from the late second century (*LSB* 864). Ambrose, bishop of Milan in the fourth century, wrote many hymns that are still used today (e.g., *LSB* 332). Congregational hymn-singing mostly died out in the Middle Ages, but was revived by Lutherans, who translated Latin hymns and wrote fresh texts. Lutheran hymnals are dominated by the classic Lutheran chorales of the sixteenth and seventeenth centuries; but they are also filled with hymns from the Early Church, the Middle Ages, modern times, and from cultures around the world.

A hymn text well-suited for use in public worship should

- be based on scriptural texts and teachings;

WHAT DOES THIS MEAN?

There is now in the New Testament a better service of God, of which the Psalm [96:1] here says: "Sing to the Lord a new song. Sing to the Lord all the earth." For God has cheered our hearts and minds through his dear Son, whom he gave for us to redeem us from sin, death, and the devil. He who believes this earnestly cannot be quiet about it. But he must gladly and willingly sing and speak about it so that others also may come and hear it. (AE 53:333)

TECHNICAL STUFF

Chorale is a technical term for the classic Lutheran hymn that arose in the early years of the Reformation. It has solid doctrinal content, is suited to a specific place in the liturgy or season, and is usually wedded to a sturdy and rhythmic tune.

- clearly distinguish Law and Gospel;
- be centered on Christ;
- teach the faith in its fullness;
- be suited to a particular place in the liturgy or Church Year; and
- offer prayer, praise, and thanksgiving to God for what He has done.

The music of our hymns also comes from all ages and cultures. We have medieval plainsong tunes, medieval carols, sturdy Reformation chorales, Genevan psalm tunes, folk tunes, and new compositions with tunes from dozens of countries including Germany, England, Wales, Sweden, Tanzania, and China.

A hymn tune well-suited for use in public worship should

- be simple enough for most people to sing, but sophisticated enough to endure;
- suit the words in mood and style;
- fit well with the rest of the hymns and liturgy;
- have no unsuitable cultural associations; and
- neither distract from the message of the words nor overwhelm it.

To satisfy these needs, musicians in the history of the Church have usually chosen to write music specifically for church use. While at times, the music of the Church has been similar to the music of the culture, this is because the culture was mainly Christian. The music of liturgy and hymns in *LSB* is in a distinct churchly form suited to an experience that is not of this world.

The Music of the Choir

In Lutheran thinking, the choir isn't part of the clergy, nor a special performing troop, but part of the congregation. It has been defined as "one or more people who can carry a tune"—thus, the choir need not be filled with professional musicians!

At the very least, the choir is a group of musically competent people from the congregation who practice ahead of time.

The choir's role isn't to offer entertainment to the congregation (as to an audience). While they prepare diligently and strive to do their best, the choir isn't offering a performance. Rather, the choir serves the liturgy by taking three important roles:

1. The choir helps the congregation in their singing of the liturgy. The choir can help them learn new (and more complex) hymns. They might sing stanzas in alternation with the congregation, particularly in long hymns. They may learn new musical settings of the canticles to add variety or teach them to the congregation. Or they might sing verses of the Psalm responsively.
2. The choir can bring richness and variety to the service by singing propers such as the Introit, Gradual, or Verse, which might be complicated or distracting for the congregation to sing.
3. The choir can bring beauty to the congregation's doxology by singing attendant music. Motets, anthems, Passions, and cantatas are historic choir pieces meant to enrich the liturgy and aid the congregation in their meditation on God's Word.

The Music of the Pastor

Historically, it was normal for a Lutheran pastor to sing his parts of the liturgy. In recent generations, many Lutherans grew unaccustomed to hearing this. The rather odd idea that he would speak and the people would sing back may have been encouraged by the fact that *The Lutheran Hymnal* put the pastor's music in a separate book. More recent Lutheran hymnals have put the pastor's music into the pew edition to remind everyone that while he doesn't have to sing his parts, it's as natural as the congregation's own song.

We sometimes use the word *chant* to describe the pastor's singing—but in reality, the congregation chants too. Any time the music provides just a simple way for a prose text to be sung (without a clear melody), that's chant. If the pastor is able, it makes sense that he sings his parts when the congregation sings theirs, especially in dialogue such as the Salutation or the Preface. In some parts of the liturgy (e.g., the Proper Preface or Consecration), the hymnal provides the pastor with rather elaborate chant music. Done well, chanting these parts can add heavenly beauty to the liturgy. But like so many other aspects of the liturgy that we call "ceremonial," there is freedom to chant or not to chant.

The Musicians

As we've noted, the Levites played many sorts of instruments in the temple worship. There is much debate in the Church today about what kinds of instruments are suitable for the liturgy. Certainly there's no divine command to use the pipe organ! But before giving up on this "king of instruments" too quickly, we should think about its advantages. It's a powerful instrument that allows one musician to lead a large congregation. It's a melody instrument that can clearly project an unfamiliar tune. It has a greater diversity of sounds available than on any other instrument. Given proper care, it is durable enough to last for centuries. And in our society, it's mostly devoid of non-Christian cultural associations.

Yet it's becoming increasingly difficult for congregations to find an organist. Other instruments can be extremely good at leading the congregation, especially if they are capable of projecting the melody clearly. A trumpet, for example, does a great job at this, while a guitar is better suited to accompanying music that the people already sing confidently. A piano provides excellent accompaniment because it provides melody, harmony, and rhythm. Electronic keyboards can be useful if they are high quality and suitably amplified.

Modern technology provides the possibility of musical leadership through recordings. This can be a great solution for congregations with no available musicians—though it takes a lot of work to prepare and isn't sensitive to the needs of live congregational singing. Too slow or too fast is often the complaint.

In this modern era, we should be cautious of purely practical solutions. We ought to treasure the God-given gifts of Christian musicians and remember that their work is more than practical. It is an act of worship.

NEED TO KNOW

The sign of the cross is made by touching the forehead, the chest, the right shoulder, then the left shoulder. In *LSB*, the symbol ☩ marks appropriate places to do this.

Gestures

A visitor from another denomination once commented to the pastor, "You Lutherans sure have a lot of audience participation!" What surprised him was the standing, sitting, kneeling, and walking, when in his church, the congregation mainly just sat.

Just as music can move the soul and emotions, so also can our bodies. God has called us to worship Him not only with our minds but also with our hands, feet, and heads. He has redeemed our bodies by washing them in Holy Baptism and feeding them with Christ's body. When the Bible speaks of "spiritual worship" or "spiritual sacrifices" (1 Peter 2:5), it doesn't exclude the body, but means that worship in body and soul is inspired by the Holy Spirit.

The most important bodily act of worship in the Bible is **kneeling** or even prostration (falling to the ground on one's face). Kneeling expresses humility, repentance, supplication, and adoration of the God who is truly present before us (Matthew 17:14; Acts 21:5; Philippians 2:10). We may kneel in the liturgy for confession of sins, prayer, and reception of the Lord's Supper. **Bowing** the head at the name of Jesus or during moments of adoration (like the consecration) is an abbreviated kind of kneeling.

FROM THE BIBLE

I appeal to you therefore, brothers, by the mercies of God, to present your bodies as a living sacrifice, holy and acceptable to God, which is your spiritual worship. (Romans 12:1)

Standing can also express belief in God's presence. Just as we stand to show respect when a monarch or president enters the room, so we stand in the liturgy, because we're in the house of the heavenly King. In Revelation, the heavenly hosts stand around the throne of God to praise Him (Revelation 7:9–12). So in the liturgy, we stand for songs of praise, the reading of the Holy Gospel, and for prayer.

Sitting is appropriate for parts of the service where we receive teaching—for the first two readings and the sermon. Because traditional Lutheran hymns are quite didactic—teaching God's Word—we normally sit to sing them. However, it can be helpful to stand for hymns of prayer or praise, and for the final, doxological stanza of a hymn (marked by △).

A **procession** is a festive act that normally also has a practical purpose. So the clergy or choir may process to their places at the beginning of the service and out at the end. The procession is led by a cross, perhaps with torches, to symbolize our following of Jesus (Matthew 16:24). Sometimes a procession brings the Holy Gospel into the middle of the congregation to symbolize Christ's incarnation and presence among us. On Palm Sunday, a procession reenacts Jesus' triumphal entry into Jerusalem.

The **sign of the cross** is an ancient devotional gesture described by Church Fathers already in the second century. The Christian first receives the sign at Baptism, when the pastor marks the candidate on the forehead and chest as one redeemed by Christ the crucified. Baptism unites us to Christ's death and resurrection (Romans 6:3–6). When you mark yourself with the sign of the cross, you are tracing over its invisible mark and recalling your Baptism. In the liturgy, the sign of the cross accompanies the holy name of Jesus in the trinitarian Invocation and Benediction, the last phrase of the Creed, and the consecration of the Communion elements.

When praying, Christians have traditionally clasped their hands together, indicating their helplessness before God. The ancient ***orans*** ("praying") posture involves extending the arms forward with the palms facing upward to God in the expectation of receiving a great gift (1 Timothy 2:8).

Study Questions

1. Why is the crucifix a central element of Christian art?

2. Why do we build churches with the altar in the east end, or at least act as if it is in the east?

3. Why do liturgical leaders wear *white* robes?

4. What was King David's central role in establishing the musical life of Old Testament worship?

5. Why is music so central to Christian worship?

6. Is it the choir's job to entertain the congregation? If not, what is its role?

7. How can we express what's happening in the service by our bodily posture?

8. What does making the sign of the cross confess?

Discussion Questions

1. Look around your church. What pieces of furniture are used for the liturgy? What is the purpose of each one?

2. What kind of vestments does your pastor wear each Sunday? What message do you think the vestments proclaim to the gathered congregation? How and why might care for the pastor's vestments be a congregational responsibility?

3. What are your favorite hymns? Why? Discuss the need to balance *likeability* with *suitability*. In other words, what makes a hymn different from a song? What makes a *good* hymn?

4. Consider the kind of music used in the five settings of the Divine Service in *LSB*. In what way is church music distinct from the music of the world? Is this a good or a bad thing?

5. What can your congregation do to provide suitable and useful instrumental accompaniment to the liturgy?

PART FOUR

What you'll learn about:

- How Old and New Testament saints prayed daily
- The way the hours of prayer connect us to the Passion of Jesus
- The daily pattern of public prayer in the Church
- How the hymnal is a helpful resource for personal devotions

God Calls Us to Daily Worship

The Divine Service is the central act of worship in the Christian Church. But worship doesn't end with its Benediction. God calls us to hear His Word and pray to Him every day. This can happen in private or with the gathered congregation. In fact, the Christian's whole life ought to be devoted to God's worship (Romans 12:1).

CHAPTER 9

Daily Prayer

In This Chapter

- The biblical roots of daily prayer
- The history of the daily office in the Church

FROM THE BIBLE

Evening and morning and at noon I utter my complaint and moan, and He hears my voice. (Psalm 55:17)

Biblical Roots

As we've seen, worship at the Jerusalem temple centered on morning and evening sacrifices each day (Exodus 29:38–39), accompanied by prayer and praise (1 Chronicles 23:30–31). God's Old Testament people synchronized their personal prayer and their synagogue services to these sacrifices by praying toward Jerusalem morning and night (Psalm 141:2). Prayer at noon completed the pious Israelite's threefold daily cycle (Psalm 55:17; Daniel 6:10).

Early Jewish Christians maintained the habit of prayer three times a day: at the third hour after sunrise (Acts 2:15), at the sixth hour (10:9), and at the ninth hour (10:30). In this way, devout people could be said to pray "continually" (10:2). St. Paul prays for the congregations under his care at specific times (Ephesians 1:16). When he writes, "Pray without ceasing" (1 Thessalonians 5:17), he probably means "at the regular hours of prayer each day."

Jesus Himself maintained a discipline of regular prayer and urged us to pray ceaselessly (Luke 18:1). But early Christians were most strongly influenced by His Passion. The Gospels record specific events during Jesus' crucifixion at the third, sixth, and ninth hours (Mark 15:25; Matthew 27:45–46). Prayer at these hours was an opportunity to meditate on Jesus' suffering for us.

Pious Personal Prayer in the Early Church

The early Christian writing, the *Didache*, urged Christians to pray the Lord's Prayer three times a day, following the Jewish pattern. By the second century, some

Church Fathers were encouraging a more thorough discipline. In addition to the third, sixth, and ninth hours, they called for prayer at sunrise and sunset, giving thanks to God for light and rest as gifts in Christ.

Hippolytus in the early third century added two more, calling for Christians to rise at midnight to watch and pray (Matthew 25:6) and a few hours later at cockcrow—remembering Peter's denial of Christ (26:74). In this way, they established a rigorous discipline of seven daily hours of prayer, commemorating the way of salvation in Christ.

TECHNICAL STUFF

Office comes from a Latin word meaning "duty" or official ceremony. The seven hours of prayer were official responsibilities of monks and ministers in the Middle Ages.

Cathedral Office

That sevenfold pattern was taken up only by those who were particularly devout—and it was quite impossible for Christians who were day laborers. For them, Hippolytus describes a pattern of public Christian gatherings each morning before work and each evening afterward. These public gatherings were perilous while Christianity was in danger of persecution. But after the conversion of Constantine, these "cathedral offices"—daily prayer in the morning and evening under the leadership of the bishop—came fully into the open.

TECHNICAL STUFF

The words *monastery* and *monk* come from Greek and Latin words meaning "alone" and refer to the way the monks withdrew from public life.

The cathedral (or people's) office focused mainly on praying the Psalms, just as the temple sacrifices were accompanied by psalm singing. The bishop might preach a sermon, and the people devoted themselves to prayer.

Monastic Hours

In the fourth century, after Emperor Constantine's conversion, the Church was suddenly flooded by new converts. Some pious Christians were put off by the apparent hypocrisy of many new Christians and began to withdraw from public worship. Put quite simplistically, this is the origin of monasteries. Some "monks" went out into the wilderness to be completely alone with their prayers. Others formed communities in the cities where they followed a "rule" and saw themselves as servants of the Church in prayer and good works. They often connected

TECHNICAL STUFF

Canon comes from the Greek word for "rule." Monasteries were ordered by a manual of instruction called a rule that ordered their canonical life.

themselves to the cathedral and prayed extra hours in between the two cathedral offices.

In this way, the sevenfold pattern of prayer that was followed by pious Christians in the early centuries developed into a system of "monastic" or "canonical hours." The most famous and influential rule was written by St. Benedict in the sixth century. He describes a pattern of seven or eight "hours" that became standard throughout the Middle Ages:

	Hour	Meaning	Time
1.	Vigil or Nocturns	"watch" or "night"	midnight
2.	Lauds	"praise"	cockcrow
3.	Prime	"first"	sunrise
4.	Terce	"third"	mid-morning
5.	Sext	"sixth"	noon
6.	None	"ninth"	mid-afternoon
7.	Vespers	"evening"	before supper
8.	Compline	"completion"	before bed

St. Benedict saw these "seven hours plus one" as a fulfillment of the Psalms (119:62, 164) and a way to "pray continually." Later in the Middle Ages, Vigil and Lauds, which often ran together, were combined into one office called **Matins** ("morning").

The major feature of the canonical hours was the singing of psalms. Benedict's Rule provided for all 150 Psalms to be sung each week. The services also included lengthy continuous readings of Scripture, hymns, canticles, and prayers.

FROM THE BIBLE

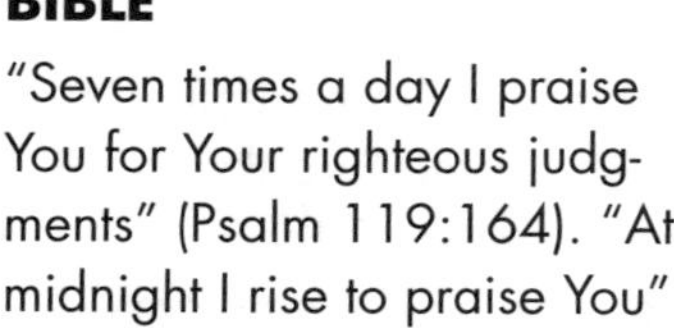

"Seven times a day I praise You for Your righteous judgments" (Psalm 119:164). "At midnight I rise to praise You" (Psalm 119:62).

Restoring Daily Prayer to God's People

Like the Mass, the daily office remained in Latin throughout the Middle Ages. Monks, ministers, and schoolchildren could understand what was going on, but the common people could not. (The rosary—a set of beads to help count cycles of praying the Hail Mary, the Lord's Prayer, and the Doxology—developed as a simple lay alternative.) Lengthy readings from the lives and writings of saints began to replace Scripture. And the new doctrine of purgatory led to private masses and prayers for the dead that got in the way of the daily office. Like the Mass, the daily office was ripe for reform.

When the Lutheran Reformation closed the monasteries, Luther saw the opportunity to restore the old cathedral office to the people. He was particularly concerned about schoolchildren. He gave detailed instructions for how Matins (in the morning) and Vespers (in late afternoon) could again become services centered on psalmody, Scripture, preaching, praise, and prayer.

WHAT DOES THIS MEAN?

Although these daily services might not be attended by the whole congregation, the priests and pupils, and especially those who, one hopes, will become good preachers and pastors, should be present. (AE 53:13)

Luther got rid of readings from the saints and restored lengthy readings of Scripture: from the New Testament at Matins and the Old Testament at Vespers, with sermons on both. At certain times of year, there were sermons on the catechism to prepare young people for their first Communion—which is the origin of Luther's Large Catechism. He wanted the whole Bible read through and all the Psalms prayed, though no more than three psalms per service. He kept the responses and the canticles; he was particularly fond of the Te Deum and Magnificat! He included German hymns and concluded with the Lord's Prayer, Collects, and the Benedicamus.

Because Luther kept much of Matins and Vespers in Latin—for the sake of the schoolchildren—they eventually declined in popularity, as Latin lost its place at the heart of education. The Common Service (1888) put Lutheran Matins and Vespers into English for the first time, borrowing translations from the Anglican *Book of Common Prayer.*

Today these services are a rich resource for schools, seminaries, and universities. Congregations may use Matins to open Sunday School, as a preparation for the Divine Service on Sundays, or as a setting for daily prayer. Like the Service of Prayer and Preaching, Matins can be an ideal setting for preaching in congregations that have not yet restored every-Sunday Communion. Vespers is well suited for Advent and Lenten services, and for the eve of festivals. Individuals will find them quite helpful for their personal daily prayer, perhaps with the aid of *Treasury of Daily Prayer* (CPH).

Study Questions

1. How did Old Testament prayer times connect to the temple?

2. How can daily prayer help us to focus on the Passion of Christ?

3. Why did morning and evening prayer become more important than the other five hours of prayer in the Early Church?

4. How did medieval monks apply Psalm 119:62, 164 to their "canonical hours"?

5. How did Luther reform the daily offices to make them more useful for the Christian congregation?

Discussion Questions

1. Look through *LSB*, pages 294–98. How might you use "Daily Prayer for Individuals and Families" in your home or at church?

2. Look at *LSB*, pages 299–304. What are the benefits of using a daily lectionary and table of psalms for your daily devotions?

Visit lutheranism101.com to download the free Leader's Guide.

CHAPTER 10

Matins and Vespers

In This Chapter

- Learning the pattern of the daily office
- Seeing the biblical heart of Matins and Vespers
- Treasuring these resources for personal prayer

FROM THE BIBLE

It is good to give thanks to the LORD, to sing praises to Your name, O Most High; to declare Your steadfast love in the morning, and Your faithfulness by night. (Psalm 92:1–2)

FROM THE BIBLE

Weeping may tarry for the night, but joy comes with the morning. (Psalm 30:5)

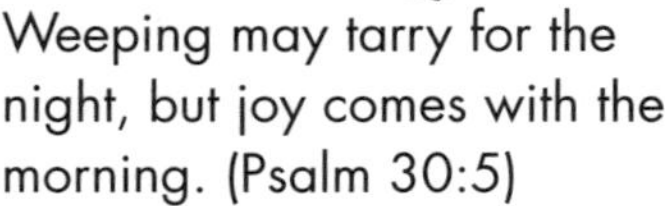

Finding Their Place

The daily office radiates out from the Divine Service like spokes from the hub of a wheel. As worshipers go forth from the Divine Service, the offices mark the hours of the day and the days of the week as belonging to God. They give rhythm to daily worship and bring us back to the Divine Service on the next Sunday. They sanctify ("make holy") daily life with God's Word and prayer (1 Timothy 4:5). Within the ancient sevenfold office, the morning and evening services hold a special place. They are the hinges on which daily prayer turns, opening and closing the day with God (Psalm 92:1–2).

Matins and Vespers have distinct moods and themes. As the morning office, **Matins** is characterized by *praise and joy* (Psalm 59:16–17). This comes through in the opening versicle ("and my mouth will declare Your praise"), and the character of the morning office hymns (e.g., *LSB* 875) and canticle (Te Deum). The closing Collect prays for God's help throughout the day. Matins celebrates the dawn as a symbol of Christ's resurrection (Luke 1:78; Mark 16:2).

Vespers is characterized by the peace that comes when we go to our rest in God's care (Psalm 4:8). The canticle (the Magnificat) is subdued and the final

Collect prays for "that peace which the world cannot give." Vespers gives thanks for evening as a promise of eternal rest in the face of death.

When Matins and Vespers are used as the "cathedral office"—as preaching services—it is appropriate for the pastor to lead. But unlike the Divine Service, the daily offices don't always need an ordained minister to preside. In the absence of the pastor, they might be led by a church elder. In a meeting, they can be prayed together. In a school, they might be led by a teacher. At home, the father of the household may pray them with his family. They are then more like devotions than public services.

FROM THE BIBLE

In peace I will both lie down and sleep; for You alone, O LORD, make me dwell in safety. (Psalm 4:8)

Finding Their Flow

The outline and flow of the daily office is different from the Divine Service. Although each of the seven historic offices was unique, they shared a basic structure. So while Matins and Vespers seem to be different services, they follow the same order, filling each section according to their distinct themes.

Like the Divine Service, the daily office provides a careful balance of sacramental and sacrificial elements. The Psalms, which are the dominant feature, are God's Word to us and provide us with God-pleasing words of praise. The office hymn offers praise in response to the Psalms. The Scripture readings are the main sacramental element, where God speaks to us. We respond to God's Word with praise in the Responsory and Canticle. Closing with prayer, we cling to His promises and call on Him for help.

DAILY OFFICE
Psalms
Office Hymn
Readings & Responsory
Canticle
Prayers

MAKING CONNECTIONS

The pattern of the daily office can help you form your personal devotions, whether or not you follow Matins and Vespers in full. Pray a psalm, sing a hymn, read the Scriptures, and pray. This pattern gives the first word to God and grounds your praise and prayer in what you've heard from Him.

Daily Offices in *LSB*

LSB provides the orders of **Matins** (p. 219) and **Vespers** (p. 229) in their traditional Lutheran form. The music consists mostly of simple Anglican-style chant tones, sometimes in four-part harmony. In the

MAKING CONNECTIONS

Luther meant for his Small Catechism to be a devotional resource. It contains morning, evening, and table prayers (*LSB*, pp. 327–28). In addition to orders of service, a hymnal such as *LSB* provides psalms, hymns, and prayers for family and personal devotions.

1970s, two new services were prepared: **Morning Prayer** (p. 235) and **Evening Prayer** (p. 243). These aren't really different orders, but Matins and Vespers with new translations of the texts and new musical settings. We'll note a few other differences below.

Early Lutherans also retained the later evening service called **Compline**. *LSB* (p. 253) contains a version that's very close to the medieval form. It's briefer and more contemplative than Vespers and isn't meant to contain a sermon. Pray it and go straight to bed!

Finally, *LSB* offers four brief daily orders without any music that could be thought of as modern versions of the minor canonical hours. **Daily Prayer for Individuals and Families** at morning, noon, early evening, and close of day (pp. 294–98) contain the same basic elements as Matins and Vespers but are much simpler.

Psalmody

The Psalms hold an even more significant place in the daily offices than they do in the Divine Service. In the Middle Ages, Matins could contain a dozen or more psalms, spread throughout the service. Luther's reform suggested using no more than three. In *LSB*, the Psalms are grouped at the beginning of the daily offices. The Psalms are God's Word to us—but they're not so much instruction or proclamation (like the other Scripture readings) as they are divinely given words of prayer, praise, and thanksgiving. God provides us with the words to speak back to Him, and so we can be sure that He's pleased.

Since King David was the principal author of the Psalms and Jesus is the Son of David, it's Jesus' voice that we hear in this book. When we sing the Psalms to God, we do so through Jesus, who takes up our song and presents it to our Father. While some psalms are clearly prophetic of Jesus, all of the Psalms are Christ's own song. Our praise is His praise, our lament is His lament, our prayer is His prayer.

Psalms appear at the beginning of the daily office in three ways.

Opening Versicles

The **Opening Versicles** of Matins and Vespers are simply psalm verses. "O Lord, open my lips, and my mouth will declare Your praise" (51:15) is uniquely suited to Matins. When we arise in the morning, we call on God to give us words of praise. Unless He first comes to us, we can't worship Him. Originally, Vespers began with just the next versicle, "Make haste, O God, to deliver me" (70:1). It was a prayer for God's help in the face of coming darkness, but it applies equally to the coming day. At one time, Psalm 70 was sung in its entirety as monks processed to the chapel.

We sing the **Gloria Patri** after the versicles as we do in singing all psalms. It reminds us that the Psalms are addressed to the triune God and gives us biblical words to praise Him.

NEED TO KNOW

A "versicle" (meaning "little verse") is a brief biblical statement, usually half a verse from the Psalms. Another part of the congregation replies with a "response," the other half of the verse.

Evening Prayer contains at this point the ancient **Service of Light** (Latin: *Lucernarium*). This is based on an ancient ceremony in which many candles were lit as darkness approached to remind us that "Jesus Christ is the Light of the world." A large candle representing Christ is carried into the church during the opening versicles to symbolize the incarnation (John 1:9). The **Phos Hilaron** (Greek for "joyous light") is an ancient evening hymn. The **Thanksgiving for Light** picks up on many Old Testament images of God's light fulfilled in Christ.

Ordinary Psalm

Matins continues with the **Venite** ("come!"). While we might think of the Venite as a canticle, it's really just selected verses from Psalm 95, which provides a perfect opening for the day: "O come, let us sing to the Lord." The Venite is an "ordinary psalm," always sung at Matins before any others. The traditional way for Christians to sing psalms involves selecting a theme verse to be sung before and afterward, called an "antiphon." The antiphon for the Venite is called the **Invitatory** because it "invites" us, saying, "O come, let us worship Him."

Vespers in *LSB* doesn't have an ordinary psalm. But Evening Prayer includes the traditional evening psalm, **Psalm 141**, beginning, "Let my prayer rise before You as incense, the lifting up of my hands as the evening sacrifice." These words remind us that in the Old Testament, evening prayer was carried out while lamps were lit, incense was burned, and animals were sacrificed at the temple. For us Christians who remember the once-and-for-all sacrifice of Jesus, it reminds us that He lifted up His hands for us (on the

FROM THE BIBLE

When Aaron sets up the lamps at twilight, he shall burn it, a regular incense offering before the LORD throughout your generations. (Exodus 30:8)

cross) and that we can approach God in prayer because of His sweet-smelling sacrifice.

Additional Psalms

After these "ordinary psalms," the daily office calls for one or more **psalms** to be sung. Traditionally, Psalms 1–109 were used in the morning and Psalms 110–150 in the evening. But psalms may also be chosen because they fit the season of the Church Year or the readings. Or we simply sing through the Psalms in order, ending each with the Gloria Patri.

The Psalms are Hebrew poetry. Rather than rhyming, Hebrew poetry is characterized by parallelism. This means that each line is normally divided into two parts that say the same thing in different words or draw a contrast. So psalms are ideally suited for responsive or antiphonal speaking or singing. While it can be meditative to speak the Psalms, they are really meant to be sung. There are many different ways to do this:

- between two groups in the congregation such as left and right sides or men and women;
- between the choir and the congregation;
- between the liturgist and the congregation; or
- in unison.

There are also many different musical settings available:

- simple chant tones for one or two verses at a time (*LSB*, p. xxvi);
- more elaborate choir settings with a congregational antiphon; and
- hymn paraphrases.

FROM THE BIBLE

And walk in love, as Christ loved us and gave Himself up for us, a fragrant offering and sacrifice to God. (Ephesians 5:2)

WHAT DOES THIS MEAN?

The whole Psalter, Psalm by Psalm, should remain in use, and the entire Scripture, lesson by lesson, should continue to be read to the people. (AE 53:38)

MAKING CONNECTIONS

See *LSB*, p. 304, for suggested psalms. *LSB* only provides psalms that are included in the lectionary. To pray through all 150 Psalms, as was traditionally done in the daily office, you can use a Bible or a special edition of the Psalter.

Office Hymn

The **Office Hymn** follows the Psalms as a human response to those divine hymns of praise. Like the Psalms, they usually end with a trinitarian doxology. The Office Hymn is meant to fit the time of day, though it can also suit the season of the Church Year or the theme of the readings. It normally has the character of praise or prayer.

Many of the morning and evening hymns in *LSB* were written originally to be sung in the daily office in monasteries. Some of them are the most ancient hymns in the hymnal, dating back to the fourth century (e.g., *LSB* 874). By the end of the Middle Ages, there were more than ten thousand office hymns in use, mostly written in Latin. The Lutheran Reformers (and later Anglicans) treasured this heritage and translated many of them for congregational use.

NEED TO KNOW

"Antiphonal" refers to a style of liturgical singing in which two parts of the congregation sing back and forth by whole or half verse. "Responsive" normally means between the liturgist and the congregation.

WHAT DOES THIS MEAN?

Some daily lectionaries take you through the whole Bible in one to three years. You could read continuously through the Old Testament in the morning and the New Testament in the evening—or vice versa. *LSB*, p. 299, provides a one-year daily lectionary that fits the seasons of the Church Year to keep your daily devotions connected to the Sunday service.

Scripture Readings

God's Word is the chief "sacramental" element of the daily office. Everything we have said about the importance of the Scripture readings in the Divine Service holds true for their place in the daily office. But the use of the readings is slightly different. In the Divine Service, the Holy Gospel sets a theme that is reflected in the Old Testament Reading and Epistle. The lectionary appoints readings from only some of the Bible. But in the daily office, things are more flexible and comprehensive. This is an opportunity to read through the whole Bible, to hear the full counsel of God.

On festivals, Matins and Vespers will have readings appointed that suit the theme of the day. But otherwise they follow a continuous reading of Scripture. There are many daily lectionaries available to help. When using the daily office as a congregational service, we sit for all the readings to recognize that we're receiving divine instruction.

WHAT DOES THIS MEAN?

On Monday and Tuesday mornings we have a German lesson on the Ten Commandments, the Creed, Lord's Prayer, baptism, and sacrament, so that these two days preserve and deepen the understanding of the catechism. (AE 53:68)

Responsory

The **Responsory** is, well, a "response" to the readings. It takes up biblical verses and uses them to praise God for His Holy Word (Psalm 86:11). The Responsory has a traditional pattern: two verses and the first part of the Gloria Patri are sung by the liturgist or choir; the congregation then answers each line with a repeated response. Think of it as a miniature psalm. The Responsory can change with the season to help set the liturgical mood. The Lutheran Reformation kept many traditional Responsory texts.

Sermon/Catechesis

When Matins and Vespers are used as congregational services, this is the place for a **Sermon**. Following immediately after the readings, preaching in the daily office is meant to be "expositional"—teaching, explaining, and applying the Scripture readings to the congregation. In the early days of the Lutheran Reformation, these daily services were the place where instruction in the basics of the faith was given. The head of the household brought his children and servants to church to hear sermons on the catechism to prepare them to receive first Communion. Today, some pastors still do catechesis within a Vespers service.

Canticle

What better way to respond to hearing God's Word than with a song of praise He gave? The **Canticle** is a song taken from the Bible outside the Psalms. St. Paul refers to three kinds of songs used in Christian worship (Ephesians 5:19)—perhaps psalms, canticles, and hymns. The three most important biblical canticles are found in Luke 1–2 and are connected to the birth of Jesus: the Benedictus, Magnificat, and Nunc Dimittis.

But there are more than a dozen other biblical canticles from the Old and New Testaments that were also used in the daily office (see *LSB* 925–29). Many of the great fourth-century manuscripts of the Greek Bible have these canticles collected into one place after the Psalms, telling us how important they were for Christian worship. One beloved canticle comes from the Apocrypha: "All You Works of the Lord" (*LSB* 931), the song of the three young men in the fiery furnace.

Te Deum ~ *We Praise You, O God*

The **Te Deum** (*LSB*, p. 223) is in a class of its own. Strictly speaking, it's not a biblical canticle, but it is an early Christian hymn based on Scripture that has been used in the liturgy since the fifth century. According to legend, it was composed by Ambrose and Augustine when Bishop Ambrose baptized Augustine. Verses 1–3a praise God the Father. Verse 3b is a trinitarian doxology. Verses 4–7 praise Christ by declaring what He has done in a creed-like way. In fact, Luther spoke of the Te Deum as one of the three Christian creeds! Verses 8–9 are prayer versicles attached to the Te Deum in the Middle Ages. The Te Deum was traditionally sung at Matins on Sundays.

MAKING CONNECTIONS

If Matins or Vespers is used for personal, family, or even congregational devotions, it isn't necessary to have a sermon, especially if they're not led by a pastor. Perhaps a reading from a devotional book could follow the readings, or simply a few comments on the text. Or the Scriptures can be left to speak for themselves.

Benedictus ~ *Song of Zechariah*

The **Benedictus** (*LSB*, p. 226) was sung by Zechariah when his son John (the Baptist) was circumcised and named (Luke 1:68–79). It takes up Old Testament language of praise and applies it to God for visiting and redeeming His people in the coming Messiah. From verse 5 onward, Zechariah addresses his baby son directly, speaking of his important prophetic ministry. The Benedictus was traditionally sung at Lauds, which eventually merged into Matins. Today, we use it as a seasonal alternative to the Te Deum, appropriate to Advent, Christmas, and Lent.

TECHNICAL STUFF

The books of the Apocrypha are contained in the Greek Bible but not in the Hebrew Bible. They are considered profitable to read but not divinely inspired.

Magnificat ~ *Song of Mary*

The **Magnificat** (*LSB*, p. 231) is Mary's song of praise in response to Gabriel's announcement that she was pregnant with Jesus (Luke 1:46–55). It's a paraphrase of the song of Hannah (1 Samuel 2:1–10), who received the child Samuel as a miraculous gift from the Lord. This shows how Mary was steeped in God's Word. This canticle is traditionally sung in Vespers, as it is a more subdued, quiet song of praise.

NEED TO KNOW

Te Deum in Latin means "You, God," the opening words of this early Christian canticle used in Matins.

NEED TO KNOW

Benedictus means "blessed," the first word of Zechariah's song (Luke 1:68–79). This is Old Testament language of praise. The canticle is used in Matins.

NEED TO KNOW

Magnificat means "magnifies," the first word of Mary's song of praise (Luke 1:46–55). The canticle is used in Vespers.

LSB Vespers uses Psalm 141:2 as an antiphon to the Magnificat. In the Middle Ages, seven "O Antiphons" were used on the evenings leading up to Christmas—these are the basis of the hymn "O Come, O Come, Emmanuel" (*LSB* 357).

Nunc Dimittis ~ *Song of Simeon*

The **Nunc Dimittis** (*LSB*, p. 258) is the song Simeon sang when he saw the baby Jesus at the temple (Luke 2:29–32). We've met it already as the closing canticle in the Lutheran Divine Service. But its more common place is in the nighttime service of Compline. By singing it before going to bed, we confess that we are unafraid of night, whether it brings sleep or death, because we have seen our salvation.

Prayers

The **Prayers** in the daily office follow a simple pattern that moves us from the most general of prayerful requests to the most specific:

- Kyrie Eleison
- Lord's Prayer
- Collect of the Day
- Other Collects
- Final Collect

This is the way God's mercy moves us. We pray for others before we pray for ourselves. We submit ourselves to God's wisdom, saying simply, "Have mercy," before we tell Him what we think we need. We express those needs in the short-and-sweet Collect pattern, rather than thinking we'll be heard because of our many words (Matthew 6:7). The final Collect expresses the character of the service: for grace in Matins and for peace in Vespers.

Blessing

The daily office traditionally ended quite simply with the **Benedicamus**: "Let us bless the Lord. Thanks be to God." If an ordained minister led the service, he would add a trinitarian **Benediction** (2 Corinthians 13:14).

Morning Prayer offers the possibility of ending with the **Paschal Blessing**.

This involves reading the Easter Gospel (Luke 24:1–7) and singing the Te Deum. This was an ancient way to elevate Matins on Sundays, which are always "little Easters."

NEED TO KNOW

Compline comes from the Latin *completorium*, meaning a service at the "completion" of the day. It was the brief office sung in monasteries immediately before bedtime.

Compline

Although the Lutheran Reformation was most concerned to keep the cathedral offices (Matins and Vespers) for the sake of preaching, Lutherans were also fond of **Compline**. The opening line sets the theme: "The Lord Almighty grant us a quiet night and peace at the last" (*LSB*, p. 253). The outline of Compline is similar to Matins and Vespers, though the service is much briefer.

Compline
Opening Versicles
Confession
Psalms
Office Hymn
Readings & Responsory
Prayers
Canticle

One unique feature of Compline is the **confession** of sins. This comes from a wise daily ritual in a monastic community: to confess the harm done to one another and be reconciled before going to sleep (Ephesians 4:26). This confession is brother to brother and sister to sister. It ends with a prayer for pardon based on trust in God's Word rather than an absolution by a pastor.

The character of Compline is peace and calm in anticipation of God-given rest. The traditional Compline **Psalms** (4, 91, 134) emphasize rest and peace. The **Responsory** connects this peace with the death of Christ, as we sing with Him: "Into Your hands, O Lord, I commend my spirit." The **Nunc Dimittis** comes just before the **Benediction**. Aged Simeon gives us the words to confess that we rest in peace through Jesus.

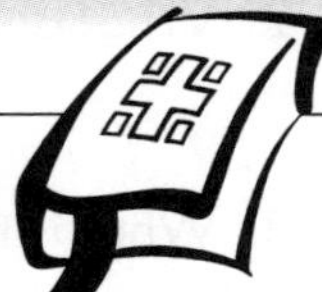

FROM THE BIBLE

Be angry and do not sin; do not let the sun go down on your anger, and give no opportunity to the devil. (Ephesians 4:26–27)

FROM THE BIBLE

Come to Me, all who labor and are heavy laden, and I will give you rest. (Matthew 11:28)

Study Questions

1. What are the distinct moods and themes of Matins and Vespers?

2. What are the five basic components of Matins and Vespers?

3. What is the role of psalms in the daily office?

4. What is the difference between how the Scriptures are read in the Divine Service and how they are read in the daily office?

5. What is a canticle? Where are the most important liturgical canticles found?

6. What is the most important canticle that doesn't come straight out of the Bible? What is the legend of its origin?

7. What did Mary probably use as the basis for composing her canticle, the Magnificat? Why is this important to note?

8. What is the pattern of prayer in the daily office? What can this pattern teach us?

Discussion Questions

1. Consider how you might make use of Matins and Vespers in your daily devotional life or in your congregation. What resources are available in the hymnal? What other helps are available?

2. Read Psalm 141 as it appears at the beginning of Evening Prayer (*LSB*, pp. 245–47). Discuss what it means when *you* are the one praying it. Then consider how its meaning deepens when you think of it as *Jesus'* prayer.

3. How might the opening confession in Compline be useful in your personal life?

4. As you conclude this study of the liturgy, consider and discuss the many ways in which you might make better use of the hymnal in your devotional life, alone, with your family, and in your church activities.

Visit lutheranism101.com to download the free Leader's Guide.

CONCLUSION:

Sitting at Jesus' Feet

I suppose we tend to think of worship as a simple idea. Worship arises spontaneously from the heart of anyone who has been touched by God. We praise God because of who He is. We thank Him for what He's done for us. We pray to Him for what we need. There are as many ways to do this as there are Christians.

Piling heavy hymnals and ponderous language and Latin phrases on top of our free and natural worship would seem to suffocate it. And, of course, the freedom Christ has given us in the Gospel should never be entirely stifled. But God's Word tells us that what comes out of our hearts isn't necessarily good and pleasing to God, because our hearts have been messed up by sin (Matthew 15:18–20). Our instincts need to be remade by God's Word.

The disciples once asked Jesus, "Lord, teach us to pray, as John taught his disciples" (Luke 11:1). They had learned from Jesus to not automatically trust what came out of their hearts. So, although we think of prayer as a natural act, the disciples wanted Jesus to show them the true way to speak to their heavenly Father—and Jesus gave them His Prayer. So also with worship. We need to question our instincts and see whether they're self-centered or God-pleasing. To find out, we need to pause and listen to the way God teaches us to worship Him in His Word.

As we've done that listening in this book, we've come across some rather complicated Latin and Greek language. We keep a bit of Latin and Greek on our tongues to remind us that we aren't the first Christians to worship God. We throw in some Hebrew words to remember our link to God's people of old. We've received the liturgy from a host of Christian witnesses who've gone before us. We sing songs of the angels to remind us that we're part of a worshiping community that spans the gap between heaven and earth.

But despite these complicated words and ideas, the Christian liturgy can be boiled down to a simple idea that's taught by the story of Mary and Martha (Luke 10:38–42). Martha sometimes gets a bum rap. We think she's done it all wrong, and Mary's done it all right. But that's not quite what the story says. Martha welcomed Jesus into her home and worked hard to serve Him a needed meal. None of this was wrong. But Jesus, nonetheless, commends her sister Mary for choosing "the good portion." Mary "sat at the Lord's feet and listened to His teaching." She recognized that Jesus didn't come to receive their service but to offer Himself to them, to bring them words of divine life.

That's what the liturgy is about. Jesus comes into our midst offering divine gifts. He's with us in person. The Divine Service is all about Him. And we sit at His feet to receive the gifts. When the time is right, He's pleased to receive our service, just as He was pleased when the women fed Him and anointed His feet and even came to prepare His body for burial. First one and then the other: Jesus comes to us with His gifts, and we receive them and return to Him our service of prayer, praise, and thanksgiving. The rhythm of worship. But always Jesus.

Glossary

Advent. From the Latin for "coming," the season of Advent focuses on Christ's first coming at Christmas, His second coming on the Last Day, and His coming in between by Word and Sacrament.

Agnus Dei. Latin for "Lamb of God," it refers to the canticle sung at the beginning of the distribution of the Lord's Supper based on John 1:29.

alb. Long, white linen robe derived from ancient Greco-Roman dress, whose name means "white" in Latin. It is the basic liturgical garment for all ministers and assistants.

Alleluia. A Hebrew word meaning "Praise Yahweh" or "Praise the Lord."

Amen. A Hebrew word meaning "it is true." It is a congregational response by which they affirm the pastor's prayer as their own. It is also added to doxologies to say, "I believe it!"

antiphon. From the Greek meaning "responsive sound," an antiphon is a thematic verse repeated before and after a psalm or canticle.

antiphonal. A style of liturgical singing in which two parts of the congregation sing a psalm or canticle back and forth by whole or half verse.

Apostles' Creed. The ancient Western creed used in the baptismal rite. It was probably not written by the apostles but faithfully presents their teaching.

Athanasian Creed. Probably written at the end of the fifth century, this detailed creed reflects the trinitarian teachings of St. Athanasius, who was at the Nicene Council in AD 325.

Benedicamus. Latin for "Let us bless [the Lord]," these words, with the response "Thanks be to God," mark the close of the Divine Service and the daily offices.

Benedictus. Latin for "blessed," the first word of Zechariah's song (Luke 1:68–79). This canticle is sung in Matins.

canticle. From the Latin word for "little song," it refers to songs drawn from the Bible, but outside the Book of Psalms (e.g., the Magnificat).

cassock. A long, tight-fitting black robe that was adopted as the ordinary street dress of clergy in late antiquity. Today it may be worn under a surplice for leading worship.

ceremony. The way in which the rite is conducted, whether elaborate or simple. It includes the use of vessels, postures, gestures, vestments, movement, and music.

chalice. From the Latin for "cup" and normally made of silver or gold, it holds the blood of Jesus for distribution in the Lord's Supper.

chalice veil. A covering for the chalice and paten that may be plain white linen or made in the color of the Church season.

chasuble. An ample round vestment developed from the ancient cloak. Made in the color of the Church season, it is worn over the alb and stole to mark the presider at the Lord's Supper.

chorale. The classic Lutheran hymn that arose in the early years of the Reformation.

Christmas. A contraction of "Christ's mass," it refers to the Divine Service in celebration of His birth.

church. The English word comes from the Greek *kyriakos*, meaning "Lord's day" or "Lord's building." The New Testament uses the word *ecclesia* ("assembly") to refer to the Church as God's people.

cincture. A rope or fabric belt worn around the waist of an alb or cassock.

Collect. A brief prayer that normally includes these parts: address, rationale, petition, benefit, doxology. The liturgist "collects" the prayers of the congregation and prays like Christ on their behalf.

Compline. From the Latin *completorium*, meaning a service at the "completion" of the day. It is a brief office to use immediately before bedtime.

creed. From the Latin *credo*, "I believe," a creed is a statement of the trinitarian Christian faith, drawn from the Scriptures and handed down through the Church.

doxology. A Greek word meaning "proclaiming [God's] glory." The Gloria Patri is the most common trinitarian doxology.

Easter. The celebration of Christ's resurrection that lasts fifty days. The English word comes from the name of the pagan goddess Eostre, who had a spring festival in pre-Christian Britain. In most other languages, the name for Easter comes from the biblical word *Pascha* (Passover).

Epiphany. From a Greek word that means "appearance." This festival and its season celebrates the revelation of Jesus to the world as God's Son.

Eucharist. An ancient name for the Lord's Supper that comes from the Greek word for thanksgiving.

fair linen. A long, rectangular white linen embroidered with five crosses (representing the wounds of Christ) that covers the top of the altar and hangs down the sides. It represents the shroud left in the tomb by the resurrected Christ.

font. A basin for Baptism normally made with eight sides to recall Christ's resurrection on the eighth day.

frontal. A decorated fabric in the color of the Church season that hangs on the front of the altar. The pulpit and lectern may also have frontals or antependia.

funeral pall. A parament that completely covers the coffin at a funeral. Normally white with cross-shaped decorative bands, it represents the righteousness of Christ that covers one who has been baptized.

Gloria in Excelsis. Latin for "glory in the highest," the opening words of this hymn of praise, which is used in the Divine Service. It is also known as the Greater Doxology.

Gloria Patri. Latin for "glory to the Father," this title comes from the first words of this "Lesser Doxology": "Glory be to the Father . . ."

Gottesdienst. A German word that means "God's service" and emphasizes that the chief purpose of the Divine Service is to receive God's gifts in Word and Sacrament before we serve Him with prayer and praise.

Gradual. From the Latin word for "step," these words of praise from the Psalms were originally sung between the readings from the steps leading up to the place of reading.

Hosanna. A Hebrew word of praise meaning "save us now."

Introit. From the Latin for "he enters," it refers to psalm verses sung during the processional entrance of the minister with his assistants.

Invocation. From the Latin for "call upon," it refers to speaking the name of our triune God at the beginning of a service.

Kyrie Eleison. Means in Greek, "Lord, have mercy!" It can be prayed on its own or spoken as a response to petitions.

lectionary. A list of prescribed readings. The three-year lectionary in *LSB* is based on the ecumenical Revised Common Lectionary. The one-year series is based on medieval systems.

Lent. From an old English word meaning "spring," it refers to the forty-day period before Easter, excluding Sundays.

litany. An ancient form of extended prayer in which the leader speaks a petition and the people voice their agreement with a brief, repeated response.

liturgy. A Greek word meaning "work for the people." Properly speaking, it refers to the Divine Service in which God serves His people with the gifts of Word and Sacrament. "The Liturgy" is also used to refer to the historic rite (order) of the Divine Service.

Lord's Day. The new name that early Christians gave to Sunday because it was the day when Jesus rose from the dead. It became their liturgical gathering day.

Magnificat. Latin for "magnifies," the first word of Mary's song of praise (Luke 1:46–55). This canticle is sung in Vespers.

Maranatha. An Aramaic word that means either "[Our] Lord has come" or "[Our] Lord, come!" It appears in many early Communion rites and was already used in Corinth in Paul's day. It expresses the twofold meaning of the real presence in the Sacrament.

mass. The medieval name for the Divine Service, probably derived from the priest's closing words, *Ite missa est* ("Go, you are dismissed").

Matins. Meaning "morning," it is the daily office (service) that takes place in early morning.

Nicene Creed. The creed adopted by the councils of Nicaea (AD 325) and Constantinople (AD 381) to reject the Arian heresy and affirm the divinity of Christ. It is the normal creed for the Divine Service.

office. From the Latin for "duty" or official ceremony, it refers to the seven daily services or hours of prayer, including Matins and Vespers.

paraments. A general name for cloth coverings on the altar, pulpit, and lectern, normally in the color of the Church season.

paten. The plate that holds the consecrated bread for distribution in the Lord's Supper, normally made of silver or gold.

Pax Domini. Latin for "the peace of the Lord," it refers to the greeting that the pastor gives immediately after the consecration.

Pentecost. Meaning "fiftieth day," it refers to the Old Testament Feast of Weeks that was fifty days after Passover and the celebration of the outpouring of the Holy Spirit on that day (Acts 2).

real presence. The teaching that the bread and wine of the Lord's Supper are truly Christ's body and blood. More broadly, it can refer to Christ's presence with us in the Divine Service through all forms of the divine Word.

rite. A carefully arranged order of service for presenting the Word and sacramental gifts of God and our responses in prayer, praise, and thanksgiving.

rubrics. From the Latin for "red," the instructions given in our service books about how to carry out the individual elements of rite and ceremony, normally printed in red ink.

salutation. From the Latin word for "greeting," it refers to an intimate dialogue between pastor and people: "The Lord be with you," "and with your spirit."

Sanctus. Means "holy" in Latin and refers to a canticle in the Service of the Sacrament. The title comes from the first words of this angelic song from Isaiah 6:3.

stole. A long, scarf-like vestment in the color of the Church season worn around the neck and hanging in front over an alb or surplice. It is a mark of office that identifies the minister as an ordained man.

surplice. A looser-fitting version of the alb developed in northern Europe to fit over a fur-lined cassock.

synagogue. From a Greek word that means "gathering together," it refers to an assembly of Jews for study of God's Word and worship.

Te Deum. Latin for "You, God," the opening words of an early Christian canticle sung in Matins.

Triduum. Means "three days." It refers to the services from Holy Thursday (the Eve of Good Friday) until Easter Sunday, which can be seen as one long observance of Christ's Passion.

versicle. A brief biblical statement, usually half a verse from the Psalms recited by a part of the congregation. Another part of the congregation replies with a "response," the other half of the verse.

Vespers. Meaning "evening," it is the daily office (service) that takes place in late afternoon or early evening.

vestments. Special ceremonial clothing worn by the pastor and his assistants to mark their office and function in the liturgy.

Words of Our Lord. From the Latin *Verba Domini*, this refers to Christ's Words of Institution for the Lord's Supper, which He continues to speak today through His called minister to bring about the real presence.